RATIONAL EXPECTATIONS

Asset Allocation for Investing Adults

WILLIAM J. BERNSTEIN

©2014

ISBN-10: 0-9887803-2-1

ISBN-13: 978-0-9887803-2-3

Ebook design by Reality Premedia Services Pvt. Ltd.
Front cover design: "Correction," by Jacob Goldstein, Robert
Smith, and Lam Thuy Vo/NPR

CONTENTS

INTRODUCTION

Two thousand years ago, a Gentile came to the two greatest living rabbis, the rivals Shammai and Hillel, and in an attempt to incite an argument between them, asked the two to teach him the whole Torah while standing on one leg. Shammai, the Antonin Scalia of ancient rabbinical thought, angrily struck the man with a stick. The more tolerant Hillel then responded, "That which is hateful to you, do not unto another: This is the whole Torah. The rest is commentary. Now go study."[1]

Investing is, in the same way, just as simple: there are risky assets, there are riskless assets, and there is an exchange rate between them. When times are good, that exchange rate is low, and when blood flows in the streets, it is high.

Oh, yes, and one more thing. Make sure, absolutely sure, that you have enough riskless assets to tide you over during the bad times, when you are the most likely to see your income fall or even lose your job. Preferably, you should have yet more than this, so as to take advantage of that high exchange rate when it shows up, as it inevitably does.

Even more simply: you must have patience, cash, and courage—and in that order. All else, as Hillel said, is commentary.

Almost two decades ago I wrote a first electronic version of *The Intelligent Asset Allocator* (henceforth *TIAA*), which McGraw-Hill eventually published in book form in 2000. At the time, I thought I was writing a how-to for the typical small investor.

I was wrong. *TIAA*'s popularity well exceeded my modest expectations, but not in quite the way I thought. The density of the book's math and quantitative exposition made it accessible to only two classes of readers: finance professionals and scientists/engineers.

I attempted to remedy that "mistake," but I only partially succeeded, with *The Four Pillars of Investing* (McGraw-Hill, 2002 and 2010). Although *The Four Pillars* reached a wider audience, my friends complained that the math still made their stomachs hurt, so I followed that book with *The Investor's Manifesto* (John Wiley & Sons, 2009), which either stripped out nearly all of the quantitative content or exiled it to optional text boxes.

In the meantime, *TIAA* has gotten rather long in the tooth, and in more ways than one. First, the quantitative tools and investment vehicles available to ordinary investors have greatly expanded since that book's publication. Second, the Global Financial Crisis of 2008–2009 (hereafter referred to as "the GFC") increased the focus on exactly what constitutes a "riskless asset." Put another way, the definition of "money" shifts during a crisis. Before the crash, for example, most investors considered short-term high-quality corporate and municipal bonds as "money." Not any longer. Third, in the intervening years finance has undergone thoroughgoing changes, the most important being a sharpening of the definition of risk. Finally, age, in at least one respect, is the friend of the investor. Over the past decade I have learned a thing or two about finance, financial writing, and myself.

In particular, I've learned that mathematical finance models, although valuable both in practice and in theory, leave a lot to be desired. Again, take the example of risk. One can come up with myriad mathematical definitions of it, but few are much better than simple standard deviation (SD), and few are as useful as the descriptive, non-mathematical concept of "bad returns in bad times."[2]

More particularly, your portfolio will, from time to time, get hammered by "statistically significant negative returns." These are almost always short-term events. The *real* risk to your portfolio, which is the long-term failure to meet your future consumption needs, comes from just four sources that fit four different macroeconomic/geopolitical processes:

- Severe, prolonged inflation of the sort that effectively wipes out fixed-income investments and can also (but not always) less severely dent stocks.
- Economic depressions that produce the opposite pattern, devastating equities while leaving fixed-income investments intact—but only those of the highest quality.
- Government confiscation/catastrophic taxation, which is more common than we might like to admit, even in developed nations, and even in the good old U.S. of A.
- Most fearsome of all, and fortunately, the rarest of all, the collateral financial devastation that is a consequence of military action.

To be sure, you can't protect yourself completely against all of these scourges, particularly confiscation and physical devastation, but it's far better to design your portfolio with these real-world possibilities in mind, rather than with the output of a black box.

It's time, then, to begin with a clean sheet of paper in the geeky high-end world of finance books aimed at those unafraid, as this book's subtitle implies, of a little math and statistics. And the subtitle also means what it says. If the terms "standard deviation," "correlation," and "geometric average" are Greek to you, or if you think that you can time the market or pick stocks, then don't buy this book. And if you already have bought it, return it, or at least give it to someone who might make better use of it. The most commonly used phrase in this book is "since you're an investing adult." What usually follows that phrase is a brief reference to the knowledge base I assume you already have. If you're looking for detailed data on the inability of active managers to add value, or descriptions of the mendacity of the investment industry, or basic financial history, once again, you'll have to look elsewhere.

Finally, while the last chapter will very roughly sketch out suggested stock and bond allocations, I'm not going to spoon feed you model portfolios aimed at every conceivable investor at every stage of life. I assume that you already know how to adjust stock allocations arithmetically downward with decreasing risk exposure or how to fold, say, an allocation of precious metals equity or REITs into your preexisting overall domestic equity policy. (Hint: proportionately decrease the original components.)

And now, we shall go study.

CHAPTER 1

ASSET-CLASS MODELS, ASSET CLASSES FOR REAL

We'll start, as I did in *The Intelligent Asset Allocator*, with the same two-asset paradigm for stock and bond returns by bringing back an old friend from that book, your boss, who also happens to be your Uncle Fred, and who offers you two curious choices for your retirement plan:

- "Bonds," which guarantee a return of 3% per year, each and every year. While this seems a generous assumption in view of the derisory fixed-income yields in the year of our Lord 2014, it serves the purposes of our analysis well and in any case is fairly close to the long-term return of that quintessential risk-free asset, the 30-day Treasury bill. (For those of you who see red when I equate T-bills with a risk-free asset: we're talking for now about *short-term* risk. If your definition of risk is the threat to real future consumption, particularly to defease your inflation-adjusted retirement needs, then the long TIPS yield is the more appropriate risk-free asset, though it has short-term risk aplenty. More—much more—in chapter 2 about the choice of risk-free asset in the portfolio.)
- "Stocks," which are more complicated. We'll resurrect

> Uncle Fred's coin toss from *TIAA*: heads you get + 30%; tails, -10%.

The *expected* return of the coin flip is the average of these two values: 10%. But it's not the annualized return you're most likely to get: half heads and half tails, which yields the geometric average of +30% and -10%, 8.17%:

$$r = \sqrt{1.3 \cdot 0.9} - 1 = 8.17\%.$$

Your wily Uncle Fred not only wants to secure your retirement, he also wants to teach you a thing or two about finance theory, namely, that risk and reward are intimately connected. If you want safety with bonds, you'll get a low return. If you want high *expected* return with stocks, you're going to have to take the risk that sometimes you'll get a lot less than you *expected*.

As we'll see in a minute, there are several ways to define risk. But no matter how you slice it, it's already apparent that Uncle Fred's stock option, which approximates the risk and return of real-world equity, is riskier than his bond option, which does the same for the universe of "safe" assets.

He knows that you're good with numbers, so you fire up Excel, brush up on the BINOMDIST function, and ask yourself just how likely it is, say, over a 30-year time horizon, for stocks to come out behind the 3% certain return of bonds.

For 30 coin tosses, how many tails must you get to fall below the 3% bond return? It turns out that if you flip only 11 heads, you will get a return of almost exactly 3.0%. The odds of flipping 11 heads are 5%. The probability of flipping 10 heads or less, and thus getting less than the 3% bond return, is also 5%. Therefore, the odds of your coming out ahead with the stock coin flip are 90%. Figure 1-1 plots the probabilities for each coin flip outcome in the shape of the classic Gaussian distribution.

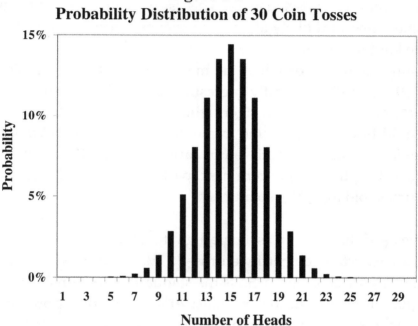

Figure 1-1
Probability Distribution of 30 Coin Tosses

Let's take a breather and consider the meaning of risk in this situation. Obviously, the most important risk to you, *in the long run*, is that the coin flip will return less than the "bond" option, and this risk (less than 11 heads) turns up 5% of the time. This specific probability, which is a statistical metaphor for the risk that you may not be able to meet your retirement spending needs, is a much more realistic and intellectually satisfying definition of risk than the standard deviation of returns is.

Almost no sentient being in this quadrant of the galaxy, however, feels "risk" in this way in his or her gut. Our evolutionary history has conditioned humans to experience risk over a shorter horizon—say the time it takes you to see yellow and black stripes in your peripheral vision and have your neurons scream *Tiger* hundreds of milliseconds before the thought even reaches consciousness. This is, in reality, how you will experience, and likely already have experienced, financial risk: the knot in your stomach you will feel each time you have your annual coin toss or when the market gyrated wildly in 2008–2009. (It's philosophically interesting to speculate whether or not a cognitively advanced tiger, which has no natural predators, would have a longer time frame of risk perception.) Standard deviation does a superb job of capturing this short-term risk. Does it capture longer-term risk, particularly that of a poverty-stricken old age? Not so much.

I've used the coin flip as a paradigm for stocks because the coin flip's expected geometric return—8.17%—is approximately the same as for U.S. stocks. So is the standard deviation (SD) of an equal number of heads and tails: 20%, versus the approximate value for U.S. stocks, which although averaging 16%, can temporarily range much higher. Two things are important about the SD. First, according to the below approximation, SD accounts for the difference between the average return of the coin flip (10%) and the annualized, geometric return 8.17%

$$G \approx A - (SD)^2/2.$$

Or, more simply,

$$G \approx A - V/2.$$

Where G is the geometric return; A, the arithmetic return; and V, the variance (which is simply the square of the SD).

The V/2 term is often referred to as the variance drag, which is a measure of how asset-class volatility reduces overall return. The classic example of variance drag is the difference between two pairs of returns: +10%/-10% and +50%/-50%. Both sequences have the same A, which is zero, but their G's are vastly different. The first sequence leaves you with $0.99 on the dollar; the second, with $0.75.

Finance sticklers insist on always using A as a measure of expected return, and, in fact, there is one type of calculation—mean-variance optimization—that we'll encounter in chapter 2, where it must be used. For everyday purposes, however, G is a much more honest return measure, since you cannot eat A in retirement, only G. Think of A as psychic income. It's nice to have, but it doesn't pay the bills.

The second, and more profound, significance of SD is as a measure of the volatility of an asset-class or security. As such, it is a measure of short-term risk. Is volatility synonymous with short-term risk? No. Is it a perfect measure of it? No, again.

But, at least as far as short-term risk goes, it's darned good. Other quantitative measures of risk are available: hemivariance (variance calculated only from below-mean values), negative skew, worst-case historical data, and so forth. For my money, the best measure of risk is more qualitatively described by academic and practitioner Antti Ilmanen, who labels it the propensity towards "bad returns in bad times."[1]

To illustrate this, consider for the sake of argument two bonds, both of which in 9 years out of 10 yield a total return of 15%, and in one year out of 10 suffer a total return loss of 50%. The expected geometric return of this series is

$$\sqrt[10]{0.5 \times 1.15^9} - 1 = 5.81\%.$$

Let's suppose that the first bond with this returns series is a "disaster bond" that suffers a 50% total return loss when a hurricane strikes a given locale and that the second bond is a high-yield corporate security that loses 50% during a financial crisis.

The junk bond, in other words, suffers its loss at just the wrong time, when the demand for liquidity is the highest—during a financial panic. It must, thus, sell at a lower price and offer a higher return than the disaster bond, whose losses will be independent of the global financial system. This is no small point: how much liquidity you have when blood runs in the streets is likely the most important determinant of how successful you'll be in the long run, since this is the time you're most likely to lose your job, need cash to purchase stocks on the cheap, or buy the corner lot you covet from your impecunious neighbor.

Contrariwise, the disaster bond provides excellent diversification value to the portfolio, since its bad return years will vary randomly with the bad returns of the more conventional risky assets that will make up the bulk of your holdings. Thus, it should be more highly priced and so offer a lower yield.

The same is also true of different stock asset classes. Those that will perform better during a crisis, particularly those that are financially strong or produce essential consumer goods (food, toilet paper, mortuary supplies) will be priced higher, and thus have lower returns, than the equity of companies that make "discretionary" products whose purchases can be deferred — autos, houses, and consumer electronics, for example.

This latter class of equities — so-called cyclical stocks, whose earnings and dividend streams are especially vulnerable during a crisis — will sell at lower prices, and thus have higher expected returns, than the overall market. Much has been made recently, for example, about the higher returns of low-beta stocks. At first blush, this seems to be a free lunch of sorts: higher returns for lower volatility. More research is needed to determine if this return factor is truly independent of the return factors we'll discuss later in the chapter.[2]

Finally, stocks that have the potential to have high returns during crises, especially inflationary ones, such as the shares of precious metals mining companies, should consequently have the lowest returns of all among equity classes, as, indeed, they have over the past half century for which we have data.

Let's now segue from the two theoretical assets discussed in the Uncle Fred and junk/disaster bond paradigms to the *actual* performance of real-world, flesh-and-blood asset classes. Some of you may want to get your fingers dirty with these data, so, first, a word or two about playing in this particular sandbox. When I started building portfolio models two decades ago, I had hoed a very tough row, begging, borrowing, and stealing from wherever I could, or worse, tediously entering thousands of monthly values from the Ibbotson yearbook into a spreadsheet.

Now, there's plenty out there for you to crunch on, and it's all free:

- Kenneth French's data library at http://mba.tuck. dartmouth.edu/pages/faculty/ken.french/data_library. html. This slices, dices, and sorts returns series for domestic and foreign stocks in more ways than you can count. It's the real mother lode, but beware. You'll need to be proficient in file management and importing non-delimited text files into Excel, since Professor French's series consist of compressed data that must be parsed out using space delimitation.
- The MSCI series of country returns. You'll have to register (for free), and learn to navigate the site. Its data series, which include returns for many individual nations, nicely complements Professor French's, which does not provide as much country-level detail: http://www.msci. com/products/indexes/performance.html. Again, some spreadsheet proficiency is required. In particular, you'll have to take the monthly gross indices and compute their monthly returns from those.
- www.finance.yahoo.com: Once more, you'll take the adjusted monthly historical gross prices (the last column in the tables) and convert those into monthly returns. On the plus side, the Yahoo! mutual fund data give you fast and easy access, via mutual funds, to a wide variety of the indices they track. (For example, since its inception in 1990, VEURX provides an excellent proxy for European stocks. ^GSPC, the symbol used on Yahoo! for the S&P 500, will yield daily returns, if you so desire, back to 1950, but it does not include dividends.) On the minus side, Yahoo! data are not error-free.
- Robert Shiller, the Keeper of the CAPE (cyclically adjusted

price/earnings ratio), maintains a spreadsheet that tracks prices and valuations of the broad U.S. market at http://www.econ.yale.edu/~shiller/data/ie_data.xls.

With that out of the way, let's start with U.S. equity returns. High-quality data begin in 1926. Table 1-1 lists the returns and SDs of the stocks in Ken French's data series for the 86½-year period between July 1926 and December 2012, sorted by size (that is, by the market capitalization: the total dollar value of outstanding shares).

Table 1-1. Returns and Standard Deviations for U.S. Stocks by Size, July 1926–December 2012

Decile	Return	SD
1 (Largest)	9.19%	17.67%
2	10.40%	20.40%
3	10.94%	21.42%
4	11.43%	22.60%
5	11.79%	23.87%
6	11.65%	24.98%
7	11.83%	26.04%
8	12.03%	28.16%
9	11.30%	30.77%
10 (Smallest)	12.59%	35.16%

Data source: Ken French Data Library, http://mba.tuck.dartmouth.edu/pages/faculty/ken.french/data_library.html.

Note how, with the exception of the deciles 5-6 and 9 returns, there's a fairly monotonous inverse relationship between return and size. A dollar invested in the smallest stocks on June 30, 1926 was worth $28,405 on December 31, 2012, whereas a dollar invested in the largest stocks was worth "only" $2,009. Note also the perfect relationship between risk and size: the smallest and largest stocks have annualized SDs of 35.16% and 17.67%, respectively.

Table 1-1 makes it look all too easy: invest in the riskiest stocks (in this case, the smallest ones), go to sleep for almost 9 decades, and you (or at least your great-grandchildren) will wake up to wealth beyond avarice. What's wrong with this picture? Lots.

- The very long-lived investor in Table 1-1 didn't spend any of the money. For each percent of annual withdrawals, the ending corpus more than halves.
- The investor didn't factor in the brokerage and advisory fees of the portfolio, which likely, particularly in the early part of the series, exceeded a few percent per year.
- Price spreads, though negligible in decile 1, increase rapidly with smaller stock size, wiping out much of the advantage of small stocks. Further, in order to maintain a portfolio of small stocks, a fair amount of trading and payment of capital gains taxes is necessitated as some of the smaller stocks grow out of their cohort each year. These, by definition, tend to be the largest positions.
- Taxes on dividends were not paid.

These four items, however, pale in comparison to what I call "semilog risk myopia." Figure 1-2 plots the value of a dollar invested in deciles 1 and 10.

Again, notice how easy it all looks. This is because in order to obtain a meaningful plot in the early part of the period, we have to display the dollar amounts over several orders of magnitude, and so have to resort to a logarithmic scale on the y-axis. Beware logarithmic scales! They hide a lot of financial mischief, a mischief that lies at the heart of how a too-bloodless, quantitative approach to saving and investing can lead you down the garden path.

Figure 1-2
Theoretical Growth of $1 in Deciles 1 and 10

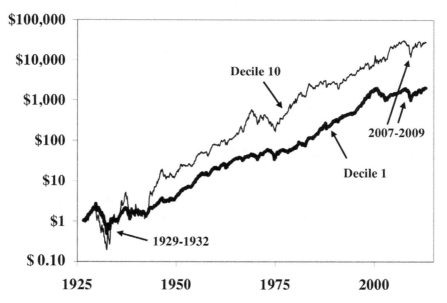

Notice the squiggles in Figure 1-2 labeled "1929–1932" and "2007–2009." These indicate the bear markets in those periods. During the most recent one, the GFC, decile 1 and decile 10 stocks lost 44.5% and 55.1%, respectively, of their value, including reinvested dividends. During the 1929–1932 bear market, they lost 81.9% and 89.3%, respectively. In the words of Fred Schwed, one of the most astute financial market observers who ever lived (and certainly the funniest),

> There are certain things that cannot be
> adequately explained to a virgin either by words
> or pictures. Nor can any description I might offer
> here even approximate what it feels like to lose a
> real chunk of money that you used to own.[3]

It is one thing to map out a portfolio strategy in a spreadsheet and quite another to execute it in the real world. My favorite analogy for this simulation/real-world disconnect is the difference between practicing in a flight simulator and flying an actual aircraft. The odds that you'll react to a simulated crash-landing better than to the real deal are overwhelming.

Three Kinds of Investors

In the next chapter, we'll discuss portfolio rebalancing—that is, the buying and selling necessary to maintain your chosen asset allocation—in some detail, but it's well to mention here how this relates to asset-class behavior. At a practical level, there are three kinds of investors. In ascending order of sophistication:

- Group 1: The average small investor, who does not have a coherent asset-allocation strategy and who owns a chaotic mix of mutual funds and/or individual securities, often recommended to him or her by a broker or advisor. He or she tends to buy near bull market peaks and sell near bear market troughs.
- Group 2: The more sophisticated investor, who does have a reasonable-seeming asset-allocation strategy and who will buy when prices fall a bit ("buying the dips"), but who falls victim to the aircraft simulator/actual crash

paradigm, loses his or her nerve, and bails when real trouble roils the markets. You may not *think* you belong in this group, but unless you've tested yourself and passed during the 2008–2009 bear market, you really can't tell. And even if you kept your discipline in 2008–2009, if the global stock markets experience another decline on the order of 1929–1932, you still don't know for sure.

- Group 3: Those who do have a coherent strategy and can stick to it. Three things separate this group from Group 2: first, a realistic appraisal of their true, under-fire risk tolerance; second, an allocation to risky assets low enough, or a savings rate high enough, to allow them to financially and emotionally weather a severe downturn; and third, an appreciation of market history, particularly the carnage inflicted by the 1929–1932 bear market. In other words, this elite group possesses not only patience, cash, and courage, but also the historical knowledge informing them that at several points in their investing career, all three will prove necessary. Finally, they have the foresight to plan for those eventualities. The last point is perhaps the most important: always ask yourself, will I really continue buying equities all the way to the bottom of a 90% market price decline?

In 1995, André Perold and William Sharpe published a seminal article that posited two kinds of investment behavior, which they labeled "concave" and "convex." Convex investors, like those in group 1, chase returns. Not all convex investors are unsophisticated. Short-term momentum strategies can be profitable, as we'll see later in this chapter, but success in this arena requires expertise, effort, and stamina.[4]

Concave investors, by contrast, rebalance. When stock prices fall, they buy, and vice versa. Perold and Sharpe's key insight was that in a world dominated by convex investors, concave (rebalancing) strategies will, in general, produce excess returns, and will also produce highly volatile security returns. In a world dominated by concave investors, convex (momentum) strategies will earn excess returns, and security prices will be sedate.

Under normal circumstances, groups 2 and 3 outnumber the denizens of Group 1, producing a regime in which modest market gains or losses produce appropriate selling or buying with narrow excursions in equilibrium price, as the majority of investors rebalance back to their equity targets (or, on a more basic level, "trim back" and "buy the dips," the latter of which slowly and inevitably evolves as the mantra of a long bull market). Recall that Perold and Sharpe noted that in a world dominated by concave investors, volatility is relatively low, as it is most of the time, particularly so as this is being written. (The VIX volatility index is an excellent measure of this. Just before this book was published, it briefly fell into the 12–13 region, whereas as the height of the GFC, it exceeded 80.)

But as market declines worsen past a certain point, those in Group 2—the ones who only *think* they can adhere to their strategy (or whose hedge funds had their leverage withdrawn)—abandon ship, which I've schematically represented in Figure 1-3.

At this point, the market becomes unstable and market prices depart rapidly downward, far more than predicted by the statistics of the Gaussian distribution implicit in the SD calculation.

It's inaccurate to say that "selling" increases during such periods. After all, for every share sold on the stock exchange, one is bought by someone else. Rather, what happens in this situation is that sellers are so highly motivated, and buyers so poorly motivated, that the equilibrium price at which those buyers can be drawn out of the woodwork declines precipitously.

Figure 1-3
As Market Falls, More Abandon Strategy

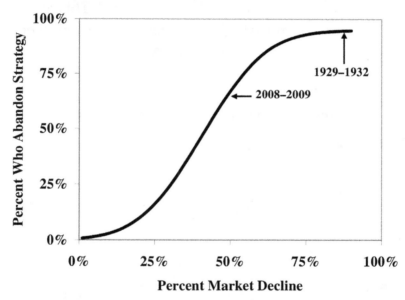

Sometimes, those falls can be dramatic. For example, the SD of the U.S. stock market, as we've seen from the above, is normally in the range of about 16%–20%. This implies a daily SD of around 1% (approximately, the above range divided by the square root of the number of trading or calendar days in the year). When, on October 29, 1987, the various market indices fell by more than 20%—that is, a -20 SD event—it clearly departed the Gaussian distribution, since a -20 SD event, at least on my spreadsheet, calculates out to a frequency of 3×10^{-89}, or about the same odds of your winning the next Olympic decathlon. (A nitpicker might point out that there are fewer than 3×10^{89} humans, but this ignores the odds that the gold medalist is reading this book.)

Rather, during exceptional downward market movements, securities distributions appear to follow the same "power-law" relationship followed by earthquakes, terrorist attacks, and terrestrial meteor/asteroid strikes, in which the logarithms of probability and of severity are linearly related. This relationship better predicts the much higher frequencies of severe events than the very low estimates from the Gaussian normal distribution.[5]

Figure 1-4
Power-Law Plot of Daily Stock Market Returns

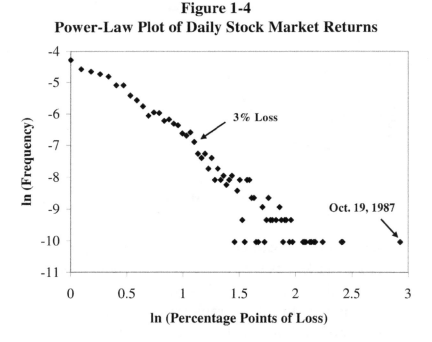

Figure 1-4 plots the daily power-law distribution of the Dow Jones Industrial Average's daily returns going back to 1926. This graph needs more than a little unpacking. First, the x-axis plots the natural logarithm of each degree of loss expressed as percentage points. For example, a loss of 3% is plotted on the x-axis at $\ln(3) = 1.1$. The frequency of such days is plotted on the y-axis. For example, a loss of about 3% (actually, any loss between 3.00% and 3.10%) occurred on 23 of the 22,881 trading days of the study period, for a frequency of 0.10%, the natural log of which plots to -6.9 on the y-axis.

Note how relatively smooth and straight the data points in the upper part of the graph are. This is because small losses occur frequently, and produce a well-behaved linear plot. The higher loss/lower frequency points in the bottom part of the graph produce a much noisier plot simply because there are so few of these rarer events. Finally, the bottom group of points lie at a y-axis value of -10, which corresponds to a frequency of 0.0044%—that is, a single trading day out of the 22,881 in the study period. The biggest outlier in this group was, of course, October 19, 1987. This relationship holds across multiple markets, and, in fact, the curves for the U.S. returns are similar to those of both the Japanese and Hong Kong stock markets.[6]

Recall the Sharpe/Perold formulation: that in a world dominated by rebalancers, momentum players earn excess return, and vice versa. Most of the time, when markets are relatively sedate, most investors *think* they're always rebalancers, buying the dips and selling when there are profits to be taken. This, in fact, produces opportunities for sophisticated investors, particularly hedge fund managers, who can play the momentum game carefully enough to avoid the high costs produced by the high turnover of a momentum strategy. At least until both their investors and their lenders lose their nerve.

But when the manure hits the ventilating system, particularly in the lower reaches of Figure 1-4 (and on the right side of Figure 1-3), the wannabe rebalancers of Group 2 give up the ghost, sell, and create opportunities for the *real* rebalancers of Group 3. The trick, then, is to design your portfolio with the nether reaches of figures 1-3 and 1-4 and of the years 1929–1932 in mind. This is easier said than done. (In actuality, momentum strategies get savaged immediately *after* a market bottom. We'll return to this phenomenon, the so-called momentum crash, in greater detail in chapter 2.)

Historical Asset-Class Returns

In the next few pages, we'll summarize the returns and risks of various domestic and foreign asset classes. As already mentioned, one of the most extensive publicly available series of returns comes from Dartmouth Professor Kenneth French's data library. Table 1-2 displays U.S. stock returns, sorted in various ways, over the 86½ years, between July 1926 and December 2012:

Table 1-2. Historical Asset-Class and Factor Returns

Panel A. Returns, SDs, and worst market losses of the "four corners" of the U.S. market between July 1926 and December 2012 sorted by size and Book-to-Market Ratio (BTM).

	Ann'd. Return	SD	GFC Loss	1929–32
Large Growth	9.34%	18.53%	-43.47%	-80.93%
Large Value	11.67%	26.06%	-58.52%	-87.91%
Small Growth	8.64%	26.88%	-52.85%	-85.44%
Small Value	14.80%	28.72%	-55.62%	-87.92%

Panel B. Sorts by various valuation measures for the U.S. market between July 1926 and December 2012.

	Low 30%	Mid 40%	High 30%	High-Low Spread
U.S. BE/ME	12.00%	14.13%	17.01%	5.01%
U.S. CF/ME	11.31%	13.80%	17.66%	6.35%
U.S. DYL	11.85%	13.38%	15.26%	3.41%
U.S. E/P	10.87%	14.21%	18.56%	7.69%

BE/ME = Book to Market (BTM)
CF/ME = Cash Flow to Market
DYL = Dividend Yield
E/P = Earnings/Price Ratio

Data source: Ken French Data Library, http://mba.tuck.dartmouth.edu/ pages/faculty/ken.french/data_library.html.

There's a lot of meat in this table, so we'll spend some time on it. First, let's define what is meant by "growth" and "value" stocks. Fama and French's (hereafter referred to simply as FF) methodology is a little obscure. The top table, Panel A, looks at stocks sorted into four "corners" by size and "valuation." Size simply refers to the size of a company's market capitalization, whereas "valuation" refers to how richly a stock is priced in the market.

The most stable measure of valuation is the book-to-market ratio (BTM, also expressed as book equity/market equity, or BE/ME), which is the inverse of the more familiar price/book ratio (P/B). As with a price/earnings (P/E) ratio, a low P/B signifies a cheap value stock, but in FF's argot, since BTM is the inverse of P/B, a value stock is one with a *high* BTM. The 30% of companies selling at the lowest/highest BTMs are growth/value stocks, that is, the most expensive/cheap. (Panel A ignores the 40% of companies in the middle.)

Panel B simply sorts stocks into three categories by valuation rather than by size. Note that all four methods of buying cheap stocks—buying only those with the highest BTM, cash flow, dividends, or highest earnings-to-market (the inverse of the more familiar P/E ratio)—produce higher returns than growth stocks. For now, don't be too concerned that some strategies appear to produce larger return spreads between growth and value stocks than others, as the pattern seen in Panel B varies from country to country and probably represents noise, not signal. Although in the U.S., sorting by E/P produces the highest spread, this is not true in other countries. And in any case, P/E is notoriously unstable and results in high portfolio turnover. If you're designing a portfolio, then BTM is the most practical metric to focus on, since it has the lowest turnover and so is the easiest and cheapest to maintain over time.

Growth stocks—think Facebook, Starbucks, Walmart, Amazon— are glamorous companies. They have hot products, rapidly growing earnings, and are on everyone's lips. In short, they are great companies. But, as you can see from the table, growth companies in general are lousy stocks. Why is this? Because everyone already knows that they are great companies, and so have bid up the price of their stocks. In fact, the buying of growth stocks generally gets overdone. There is good evidence that investors, in general, pay way too much for this earnings growth.

In a landmark paper, Michelle Clayman examined the companies profiled by Tom Peters' *In Search of Excellence* and found that in the 5 years following the book's publication, the "excellent" companies profiled by Peters returned 11% per year *less* than a matched group of "unexcellent" companies picked by Clayman using the book's selection criteria.[7]

In another classic 1993 study, Russell Fuller and his colleagues looked at the returns of stocks sorted by P/E ratio. They found that high-P/E growth stocks did not increase their earnings in subsequent years nearly enough to compensate for their high price. It's well worth examining this paper in some detail, since it so vividly demonstrates why growth stock investing is a losing proposition.

Fuller et al. started by examining the earnings and prices of stocks between 1973 and 1990. During that long-ago period, the average stock sold at just 10.2 times its earnings. The most expensive quintile (top 20%) of companies by P/E sold for 25.6 times earnings, and the cheapest quintile sold for 6.8 times earnings. Another way of putting this is that if you bought $1,000 of a total market index fund in 1973 (had one existed — the Vanguard Total Stock Market Index fund didn't open until 1992), you'd have gotten $98 of earnings. The most expensive quintile would have brought $39 of earnings, while the cheapest quintile would have brought $147 of earnings.

Thus, in order for the most expensive quintile of stocks to yield the same dollar amount of earnings as the market, it would eventually have to grow its earnings by a factor of at least 2.51 (98/39) greater than that of the overall market. To yield the same dollar amount of earnings as the cheapest quintile, it would have to grow its earnings by a factor of 3.77 (147/39) more than the cheapest quintile.

In fact, the growth stocks grew their earnings only by a factor of 1.22 relative to the market and 1.48 relative to the cheapest stocks. Furthermore, of the 22% excess growth relative to the market, 17% occurred in the first four years; only 5% came in the last four. Contrariwise, the cheapest stocks grew their earnings only about 18% more slowly than the market. Again, almost all of that deficit occurred in the first four years. During the last four years the cheap value stocks grew their earnings almost as fast as the market.[8] Figure 1-5 displays the dollar earnings generated by a $1,000 initial investment in growth stocks, $1,000 in value stocks, and $1,000 in the overall stock market.

Figure 1-5
Growth vs Value Company Earnings

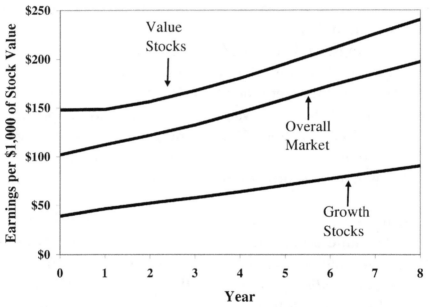

Simply put, the dollar earnings of the growth stocks never catch up with those of the overall market, and the earnings of the value stocks, whose growth does lag that of the overall market by a bit in the first four years, continue to exceed that of the market. Sooner rather than later, the excess growth of growth stocks tapers off more quickly than expected, thus disappointing their owners, and, as the hoary phrase goes, these stocks "get taken out and shot." On the opposite side of the ledger, when the earnings of value stocks begin to stabilize after several years, their prices appreciate more than that of the market and, of course, more than growth stocks.

Researchers David Dreman and Michael Berry documented this asymmetry of expectations and outcomes in a 1995 paper. When growth stocks' earnings exceeded expectations, they increased only slightly in price, but when earnings disappointed, prices fell dramatically. Value stocks, on the other hand, behaved in the opposite manner. When they disappointed, their prices fell only slightly, and when they surprised on the upside, their prices rose dramatically.[9] On a more arcane plane, Fama and French documented the same thing when they found that profitability, measured as return on equity (earnings divided by book value) of growth stocks erodes over time, while that of value stocks improves, although neither reaches the profitability of the overall market from the upside and downside, respectively.[10]

All of the above explanations of how value stocks have higher returns than either growth stocks or the overall market are, in a sense, "behavioral," as they imply that investors irrationally undervalue value stocks or overvalue growth stocks.

There's another explanation of why value stocks have higher returns, and that's risk. Value stocks tend to be more highly indebted. As a result, they are more likely to be hurt during a crisis and carry a higher risk of bankruptcy than growth stocks. This risk was realized, as already noted, in both the recent GFC and during the 1929–1932 bear market. In my opinion, both behavioral and risk factors drive the high returns of value stocks, though I'm more impressed with the behavioral story.

Outside the U.S., the growth/value dichotomy is much the same. Panel A of Table 1-3 summarizes the returns for the market, high-BTM, and low-BTM portfolios for each foreign market, while Panel B shows the sorts for BTM, cash flow/market, dividend yield, and E/P for Professor French's index of major non-U.S. stocks.

Table 1-3. The Return of Value Strategies Abroad

Panel A. Major international markets, sorted by BTM Book to Market).

Nation	Period	Market	Value	Growth
Austria	1987–2012	8.38%	12.25%	5.11%
Australia	1975–2012	12.39%	16.25%	9.24%
Belgium	1975–2012	13.06%	16.08%	13.45%
Canada	1977–2012	10.79%	11.69%	7.41%
Denmark	1989–2012	10.44%	10.95%	12.21%
Finland	1988–2012	8.74%	11.25%	9.96%
France	1975–2012	11.72%	14.38%	10.48%
Germany	1975–2012	13.39%	18.47%	12.59%
Hong Kong	1975–2012	19.30%	17.96%	17.48%
Ireland	1991–2012	7.47%	9.38%	5.33%
Italy	1975–2012	7.83%	5.44%	9.28%
Japan	1975–2012	8.29%	15.30%	3.51%
Malaysia	1994–2001	-12.71%	-8.94%	-14.72%
Netherlands	1975–2012	13.71%	13.75%	13.35%
New Zealand	1988–2012	5.63%	-4.32%	6.47%
Norway	1975–2012	11.41%	10.68%	8.23%
Singapore	1975–2012	12.42%	18.57%	9.98%
Spain	1975–2012	8.48%	7.80%	7.03%
Sweden	1975–2012	14.21%	18.37%	12.76%
Switzerland	1975–2012	12.18%	12.86%	11.66%
U.K.	1975–2012	14.21%	18.37%	12.76%
Average		10.06%	11.74%	8.74%

Panel B. Major international market index sorted by various value strategies.

	Growth	Value	Spread
Int'l BE/ME	8.80%	14.87%	6.06%
Int'l CF/ME	7.82%	14.81%	6.99%
Int'l DYL	8.34%	14.54%	6.20%
Int'l E/P	8.21%	14.42%	6.22%

Data source: Ken French Data Library, http://mba.tuck.dartmouth.edu/pages/faculty/ken.french/data_library.html.

The Umbrella Shop Theory of Financial History

Tables 1-1, 1-2, and 1-3 paint a very sunny picture of equity returns. It's important to translate these numbers into inflation-adjusted "real" returns. For example, between 1926 and 2012, the before-inflation, or "nominal," returns for the 10 deciles of U.S. stocks ranged between 9.2% and 12.6%, which, given the 2.98% inflation for the period, suggests real equity returns in the 6% to 9% ballpark. The international returns are of a similar magnitude. But there are more than a few things wrong with this picture. First, as I've already pointed out, a lot of the premiums from small stocks and value exposure are difficult to capture because of portfolio turnover and impact costs. Second, since the premiums from exposure to small and value stocks, and even the overall market itself, can now be obtained by ordinary investors with a few keystrokes, they must of necessity have decreased.

Over thirty years ago, my wife and I came upon a shop in Paris that made the most exquisite umbrellas we had ever seen.

Although their products weren't cheap, they were still within our budget. In the following few years we bought several, which we treasure to this day.

Over the subsequent years, we noticed the odd travel section article about the store. More important, with online hotel booking, growing prosperity, and airline deregulation, it became ever easier to visit Paris. No longer did we have to spend hours with a travel agent or airline reservation representative, write letters to several hotels over many weeks, carry an adequate supply of traveler's checks, and have a letter of credit from our bank, not to mention the few hundred francs to get us into town from the airport. Flights and accommodations can now be booked from our laptop, and the ATM at Orly spits out as many euros as we could possibly need. Each time we returned to the umbrella store, we found it ever more crowded with shoppers from around the world. Its prices grew correspondingly out of reach, particularly after the elderly sisters who ran the store passed it on to their tonier niece.

The same thing has happened to stocks. Fifty years ago, if you wanted to own the S&P 500 index, you were going to have to pay a broker the earth to execute each position for you. You were also likely going to pay a fee for each dividend payment. Those costs were more than well rewarded because in such a world relatively few people bought stocks. Even fewer assembled anywhere near a properly diversified portfolio approaching the S&P 500, let alone the Wilshire 5000. Consequently, since the destination was so hard to reach, relatively few made the trip, prices stayed low, and the financial rewards were correspondingly high.

Similarly, now that everyone knows about and can visit the "equity umbrella shop," stock prices have risen and lower expected returns have resulted. This likely goes double for "tilted portfolios," the term used for small-cap- and value-oriented stocks. I've already alluded to how much of a fiction some of the time series in tables 1-1 and 1-2 are. Before about 1980 or so, a diversified list of small and value stocks was nearly impossible to assemble. For example, in the late 1930s, a young John Templeton decided that small stocks were a bargain and put together a portfolio consisting of the 100 companies selling on the New York and American stock exchanges for less than a dollar per share (market cap data, in those days, being hard to come by).

He was able to do so only because his old employer, the firm of Fenner and Beane (a predecessor of Merrill Lynch), owed him some favors. Templeton made out, of course, like a bandit. He quadrupled his money in four years because almost no one else was interested in these companies.[11] Today, by contrast, anyone wanting to purchase such a tilted portfolio has her choice of ETFs and plain-vanilla funds with which to do so. But she should certainly not expect Templeton-sized returns, nor even the returns shown in tables 1-1, 1-2, and 1-3. There are simply too many customers waltzing into that particular umbrella shop.

There's another serious problem with tables 1-1 and 1-2, which is that we're looking retrospectively at one of the big winners in the global stock sweepstakes: the United States. Not only that, but we chose to begin our analysis in 1926, a superb year to start, since it just clears the awful three decades of stock returns that preceded it. (The same is also true of the international series shown in Table 1-3, which in most foreign countries begins in 1975, just after the brutal bear market of 1973–1974, but still not too late to capture much of the post-Second World War economic recovery. And as long as we're piling onto our databases, it's also worth noting that the most often cited bogey of emerging markets stocks, the Morgan Stanley Capital Indices Emerging Markets Index, begins in 1988, at the tail end of several decades of crisis in the developing world that revolved around war, debt, hyperinflation, expropriation of corporate assets, and, in a few cases, near-extinction of national stock markets, yielding fire-sale prices that paved the way for subsequent high returns.)

The widest-ranging (though not necessarily the deepest) long-term study of world equity returns in the twentieth century comes from academics Philippe Jorion and William Goetzmann, who showed that the U.S. in fact had the highest returns of any equity market, and that the real returns were in most cases mid-single digits and in some cases negative over the course of a hundred years.[12] While it's possible that the U.S. markets will also win the twenty-first-century stock sweepstakes, it would be unwise to bet on it.

What's Expected Is Not Necessarily What You Get

We start with the observation by a venerable early-twentieth-century economist, Irving Fisher, who noted that the value of any investment was simply the stream of future dividends, discounted by the risk-adjusted expected rate of return. This infinite sum can be described as follows:

$$P = \sum_{n=1}^{\infty} D_0 \frac{(1+g)^n}{(1+r)^n}$$

That is, each year the dividend grows by the factor (1+g), where g is the growth rate, but must be discounted by the factor (1+r), where r is the discount rate, which is also the expected return. By definition, the expected return has to be greater than the growth. If it weren't, the above sum would be infinite. (D_0 simply refers to the fact that our starting dividend begins in year zero.)

Though elegant, this equation is of relatively little use to us, since we're really interested in r, the return, which the above equation requires to determine price.

With a little calculus, though, we can solve this equation for r, which yields the so-called Gordon Equation,

$$r = D_1/P + g.$$

Notice how we wind up using D_1, which is the dividend after one year, having grown by the factor (1+g). From now on, we'll ignore this fine point and simplify things a bit by estimating return as the sum of two numbers, the current dividend and the historical dividend growth rate:

$$r = \text{yield} + g.$$

For those of you whose heads are spinning, there's a simpler, narrative way of arriving at this equation, which is to imagine a stock that always yields a 3% dividend, so that if the dollar amount of the per-share dividend in a given year increases by, say, 10%, then the stock price must also go up by 10%. The total return in that year is thus 13%, the sum of the dividend yield and the increase in price.

It's impossible to overestimate the power and importance of this simple formula, which lies at the center of investing adulthood. Were you to travel back in time a decade and a half to the heart of the tech bubble, you could have cleaved the suckers from the survivors by asking how they estimated future stock returns. The former would have waved their hands and talked about a technology-driven new era of high growth, while the latter's much more pessimistic answer would have sounded something like the Gordon Equation and prominently featured the market dividend yield, which at that point hovered just above 1%.

Let's apply the Gordon Equation to U.S. stocks. The place to start is Professor Robert Shiller's database, which lists prices, earnings, and dividends going back to 1871. His numbers show that for the 142-year period ending December 2012, per-share real dividends have grown at just 1.33% per year. If we look at the most recent 50 years, the number is an almost identical 1.34%. Real per-share earnings, however, have grown at a slightly higher rate: 1.76% over the 142-year period and 2.33% over the past 50 years.[13]

Let's be generous, then, and call the dividend growth rate 1.5%. As this is being written, the dividend yield of the S&P 500 is 2.1%. Add these two numbers together, and we get an expected real return of 3.6%.

The key word, of course, is *expected*. If, for example, the SD of the U.S. market is 16%, that means that the 95% confidence limits in any given year are ±2 SD, or between -28.4% and +35.6%. Keep that in mind when you hear a market strategist forecasting 8% returns next year. It's even scarier when we apply this calculation to 30-year returns. Since the SD of 30-year annualized returns is the single-year SD of 16% divided by $\sqrt{30}$, or 2.9%, a -2 SD event would result in a 30-year *annualized* real return of -2.2%. Over long periods, equity returns tend to mean-revert, so in the past 142 years the U.S. markets have never seen a real return that low. But on the other hand, we have fewer than 5 independent 30-year periods, so we shouldn't be too smug.

This gets us to another part of the return equation, the change in valuation. Let's go back and imagine that it's December 31, 1925. In that year investors had no idea about the extent of growth of dividends and earnings. In fact, the entire mathematical framework we're discussing here was unknown until Irving Fisher, Benjamin Graham, and John Burr Williams published their seminal works on the subject over the next decade and a half. (Fisher's *The Theory of Interest* appeared in 1930. Graham's *Security Analysis* was published in 1934. Williams' *The Theory of Investment Value* appeared in 1938.)

But let's make a leap and assume that investors did know about the Gordon Equation and about historical per-share dividend growth in late 1925. At that point, the dividend yield of U.S. stocks was 4.8%. Logically, then, the U.S. investor should have expected a real return of 6.3%. In fact, however, over the 74 years ending December 31, 1999, she got a real return of 8.0%. What accounted for the 1.7% difference? Simple. Between 1925 and 1999 the dividend yield fell by three quarters, to 1.1%, and the fourfold rise in the ratio of prices to dividends, annualized over 74 years, is 1.9%, very close to the observed gap between real returns and actual returns.

So we have to add an additional term, c, the expected change in the annualized change in the valuation of stocks relative to dividends or earnings due to mean reversion, to the Gordon Equation:

$$r = \text{yield} + g + c.$$

An expected increase in the dividend yield back to a historical average results in a *negative* term, and a decrease results in a *positive* term. For example, if, over the next 12 years, the dividend yield doubles, this implies a 6% annualized *reduction* in returns. (This approximation is arrived at by applying the "Rule of 72," which states that the doubling time and interest rate, when multiplied together, equals approximately 72. In this case, a 6% interest rate calculates out to a doubling time of 12 years.)

Vanguard founder John Bogle refers to the original two Gordon-Equation terms—[yield + g]—as the "fundamental return" of the market, whereas the last term, c, is the "speculative return" of the market. Over short periods, the fundamental return changes hardly at all, so day-to-day price moves are due, almost by definition, simply to the speculative return—the c term—the change in valuation. But over very long periods, the fundamental return overwhelms the speculative return. Job one for the investor, then, is to learn, as best she can, to ignore the day-to-day and year-to-year speculative return in order to earn the fundamental return.

Is there a way to estimate c, the speculative return? Day to day, or even year to year, certainly not. Since you're an investing adult, you know that no one has ever consistently called market direction over short periods. Moreover, if someone did indeed know the future direction of the market, she sure wouldn't be telling the world about it on CNBC or spilling the beans in a *Forbes* column.

Over longer periods, though, you can make probabilistic estimations of c. The classic way to estimate c, and so to more accurately estimate future returns, is Professor Shiller's cyclically adjusted P/E ratio, or CAPE. This number makes use of Benjamin Graham's observation that companies frequently manipulate or misstate earnings numbers over short periods, but that eventually this comes out in the wash, and so it is better to average earnings over the prior 5 to 10 years; Professor Shiller extended this to the earnings changes that occur over the business cycle. The CAPE, then, is taken by dividing the current index price by the average of the prior 10 years' *real* earnings of the stock market.

Figure 1-6 plots Shiller's CAPE. As of this writing, the CAPE of U.S. stocks is about 25 times earnings, well above its average value since 1881, which has been 16.5. I do think that this value is somewhat misleading, since the data underlying it begin shortly after the Civil War, a time of historically depressed security prices.

Over the past 50 years, the CAPE has averaged 19.5. If one draws a regression line through the series, it intercepts at end-2012 at 20.3, suggesting that this is closer to today's "true" fairly valued CAPE than the long-term average of 16.5. So call the "normal" CAPE 20. There are two caveats about this observation. First, if one confines the analysis to independent 10-year periods (or applies the Newey-West correction to the overlapping monthly data), as one properly should, the increase does not reach statistical significance. Second, if one eliminates the past 20 years, the tendency of the CAPE to increase almost disappears. I won't argue with the former caveat, but regarding the latter, it's never good to discard data to prove a point.

Figure 1-6
Increase in Shiller CAPE over Time

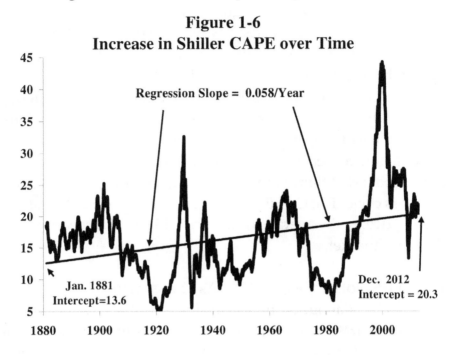

Before we go on, it's worth mentioning the different market P/Es you'll see bandied about. The most common one is the long-term average of the one-year P/E, where the E is calculated from the reported earnings of the *previous* 12 months, which is in the vicinity of 15.

People, though, tend to get very sloppy with this value, and substitute, instead, the P/E *using next year's estimated earnings.* Such estimates almost always tend to be overly optimistic and thus yield a value lower than the trailing 12-month P/E mentioned above. Others use "operating earnings" (profits minus depreciation) or, shudder, EBITDA (profits before interest, taxes, depreciation, and amortization), a measure that tends to get discussed during particularly frothy markets. Don't be fooled! The historical average, for example, of the estimated forward-year-based P/E is about 13. Any number above this suggests that the market is overvalued.[14]

So, how do we use the CAPE to calculate the third term? It all depends on your time frame. The current CAPE of 25 implies that the S&P 500 is overvalued by about 25%—that is, it would have to fall by 20% to get back to the "fair value" of 20. If you're looking forward 30 years, this annualizes out to a lowering of return by around 0.7%. If you're looking out just 10 years, this annualizes out to a lowering of about 2.2%. This lowers our 3.6% estimate to 1.4%/2.9% at 10 years/30 years. If valuations revert more slowly, then a 10-year estimate of 2% seems reasonable.

Finally, how much do we add for tilting towards value and small stocks? As already mentioned, these "umbrella shops" are now well known, and big money is chasing them. Before Fama and French described these factors in great detail in their landmark 1992 *Journal of Finance* paper, very few actively managed funds, such as the venerable T. Rowe Price Small-Cap Value Fund, pursued this corner of the equity universe.[15] Soon after, Dimensional Fund Advisors created passively managed funds aimed at these two factors. What happened next (depicted in Figure 1-7) is instructive.

This plot needs a little unpacking. It shows the value of a dollar invested in the global small and value factors. These factors are not easily investable, since they are "long-short" portfolios. The former is the return of the smallest half of the world's stocks minus the biggest half. The latter is the return, more or less, of the 30 percent of companies with the largest book-to-market ratio minus the return of the 30 percent of companies with the smallest book-to-market.

Figure 1-7
Worldwide Small and Value Factor Total
Returns

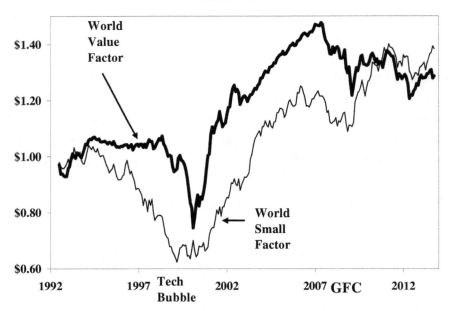

In reality, a portfolio aimed at these factors will own only the long half, so the return over the market is very approximately half of the factor return.[16] Nonetheless, Figure 1-7 demonstrates how these factors have performed in the "umbrella shop" of investing. Right out of the gate, they met up with the "new era" of the tech bubble, which favored large cap growth stocks and got clobbered. Pundits crowed about how wrong the ivory-tower folks had gotten things, which rang the bell for their spectacular outperformance between 2002 and 2007.

Both factors got hit again during the GFC. The small factor recovered after the crisis, but the value factor didn't. This was likely for two reasons. First, prior to the crisis, as an increasing number of mutual funds, ETFs, hedge funds, and private wealth managers crowded in, the umbrella shop got ever more expensive. Second, the small and value factors ran into "the limits of arbitrage," a process described by Robert Vishny and Andrei Schleifer. This is a fascinating phenomenon, and it provides hope for those who aspire to profit from returns factors of all types: older ones, such as value and small, as well as newer ones, such as momentum and profitability. In essence, over the past several decades, big institutional players increasingly manage money for less sophisticated and less patient ones. When a factor has persistent and severe negative returns, these less informed and less disciplined investors will pull money out of these institutional pools. Thus, at the very moment when future returns are likely to be highest—John Templeton's "point of maximum pessimism"—the capital that can be deployed by these institutional managers is the smallest. In the words of Vishny and Schleifer, the ability to profit from pricing factors "becomes ineffective in extreme circumstances, when prices diverge far from fundamental values. [Our model] also suggests where anomalies in financial markets are likely to appear, and why arbitrage fails to eliminate them."[17]

Thanks to the limits of arbitrage, I think that we can still expect a boost from the premiums for small, value, momentum, and profitability, but not as much as in the pre-1992 era. Although tables 1-1 and 1-2 suggest perhaps a 2% premium for small stocks and 3% for value stocks, I would count on less than half of the previous premiums at best for these two factors going forward, as well as from momentum and profitability, for the reasons mentioned above. So figure on premiums of perhaps 0.7% for small stocks, 1% for value stocks, and thus 1.7% for small value stocks. Piggybacking off the 2% estimated return of the U.S. stock market, when calculated above for the upcoming decade, this 1.7% fillip gets us close to an expected real return of 4% for small value stocks, for example.

Of course, there's always a big leap from "expected" to "realized." Since the annual SD of small value stocks has been 28.72% (Table 1-2), that means that the 95% confidence limits for 10-year annualized real returns fall between -13.6% and +21.6%. In the real world, the worst-case scenario was not nearly as bad, even taking into consideration the higher realized return. Had you been able to invest in the FF small value index at the market top of August 31, 1929, your forward 10-year annualized real loss would have been "just" 4.12%. (The nominal return would have been worse, but this was cushioned by price deflation during the period, which saw a total return nominal loss of 47.60% mitigated by total deflation of 20.21%.)

We evaluate foreign stocks in much the same way. Currently, the MSCI-EAFE index (Europe, Australasia, and Far East) yields about 3.4%, while emerging markets stocks yield about 2.4%. The second term for these two asset classes, real dividend growth, is more difficult to evaluate. During the twentieth century, the average per-share real growth rate in the developed nations for which there are data was -0.5%, but this value is skewed by the massive recapitalization needs of several war-torn economies, which produced large share dilution, and hence stunted per-share dividend growth. If we confine ourselves to nations that did not suffer large-scale destruction of their productive capacities, then per-share real dividend growth rises to +0.7%.[18] I'd compromise and estimate this second term, the g, at +0.5%.

Outside the United States, the third term, c, caused by the tendency for stock valuations to revert to the mean, yields a more optimistic picture. Financial analyst Mebane Faber has measured the CAPE of multiple national markets and come up with these numbers for the largest developed markets, expressed as long-term-average CAPE/current-CAPE: Canada, 19.9/17.3; France, 19.9/10.3; Germany, 17.9/12.1; Italy, 21.7/6.5; Netherlands, 12.0/10.0; Switzerland, 18.2/14.4; UK, 11.8/12.4.[19] Clearly, the recent European financial crisis has depressed prices, but the best fishing is usually done in the most troubled waters. Stocks never get cheap without good reason.

Eyeballing the above data suggests that, on average, developed foreign markets are about 15 to 20% undervalued, so it seems reasonable to add about 1.5% to the 10-year projection for their expected return. Thus, by adding the above 3 terms together, we come up with an expected real return of 5.4% over the next decade.

We simply do not have a good handle on long-run earnings and dividend growth in emerging markets. Mr. Faber's data show emerging markets to be fairly valued, so expected real returns in this arena are anyone's guess. One thing, however, is certain about this asset class. It can be remarkably volatile, and you'll need a cast iron stomach to include it in your portfolio. Emerging markets stocks have suffered large losses twice in the past 20 years: 56% during the Asian crisis of the late 1990s and 59% during the GFC.

Notice that we've not deemed industry groups as discrete asset classes. I believe that three of them deserve separate consideration in a portfolio: real estate investment trusts (REITs), precious metals equity (PME), and oil/base metals producers (natural resources, NR). Why do these three asset classes, among all other industry groups, deserve special attention in a portfolio?

In the past, I would have justified them, or at least attempted to, on the basis of low correlation with the rest of the portfolio components. But as the 2008-2009 bear market demonstrated, all three of these asset classes are still risky ones, and in a bad market, all will suffer sharp declines. Rather, I recommend them for more descriptive, heuristic, and historical reasons.

First, REITs. These are the shares of companies that own and operate rental properties of all descriptions, primarily offices and apartment buildings. Because, by statute, they must distribute 90% of their earnings as dividends (which are not subject to the lower preferential "qualified dividend" tax rate), they are relatively easy to value. Figure 1-8 plots the dividend rate versus their forward 5-year returns. As you can see, the dividend payout varies over a wide range and is reasonably predictive of future returns. Occasionally, such as occurred during the tech bubble of the late 1990s, their valuations can get seriously out of whack with those of the broader market. Those who invested in REITs during the 1990s tech boom, when "bricks and mortar" were considered hopelessly out of fashion, were pleased.

Because REITs can reinvest only a small portion of their earnings in their operations, their dividends grow slowly—more slowly than inflation, in fact, by about one percent per year. Since they currently yield just over 3%, their "fundamental expected return" is about 2% after inflation, and if the dividend yield reverts to the historical average of 7%, a lot less. Bottom line? Since at least some degree of mean reversion seems likely, I estimate the long-term real REIT return at around 1%.

Figure 1-8
REIT Yield vs 5-Year Return

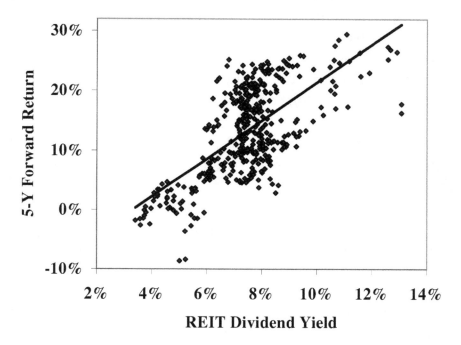

REIT Dividend Yield

Second, PME: Because the data on the dividend yields, and particularly the dividend growth rate, of the producers of gold, silver, and platinum are obscure, we are reduced to considering the historical real return of this asset class, which was 1.47% for the 50-year period ending June 2013.

Why so low? For two reasons: PME tends to do well during inflationary crises or when the public loses faith in paper currencies. This tendency to have good returns in bad times makes PME desirable. (Conversely, PME, as the GFC demonstrated, does not do terribly well in deflationary crises). PME also tends to have high prices/low returns because it is a favorite of political conservatives, who derive ideological satisfaction from owning an asset that stands in opposition to the specter of paper "fiat" currencies that can be easily debased by evil governments. For both of these reasons, the prices of PME tend to get bid up, lowering their future returns.[20] (And lest you think I'm picking on conservatives, liberals, who tend to favor alternative energy stocks and avoid the manufacturers of tobacco, alcohol, and firearms, get punished financially for their beliefs as well. Liberal or conservative, ideology and investing do not mix well.)

Third, NR: Based on standard criteria, these stocks do not represent a separate asset class, for at least two reasons. First, their correlation with the broad stock market is high, and second, they constitute a significant part of the broad market. The oil producers alone, for example, make up 10% of the S&P 500 index; in recent years, Exxon-Mobil has had, off and on, the largest market cap of any U.S. stock.

Why have a separate allocation to oil and base metals stocks when they are already well represented in the broad market index and have a high correlation to it? First and foremost, the inflation protection afforded in the overall market by these companies is largely offset by the damage done to commodity consumers, particularly airlines, railroads, and power producers, so an extra dollop of the producers does provide some protection against inflation. Table 1-4 lists the nine years since 1950 during which inflation was higher than 5% and shows the returns during those years for PME, oil, and base metals stocks, as well as the returns of the CRSP 1-10 (all stock) market index. The rows in bold at the bottom of the table list, in order, the simple average of the various asset-class returns for those 9 years; the annualized returns, as if the years had occurred consecutively; and finally, the real annualized returns for those years. Table 1-4 clearly shows that while the broad stock market does not keep pace with inflation, commodity-producing equity-asset classes— PME and NR—do.

Table 1-4. Returns of 4 Asset Classes for the 9 Years since 1950 with Inflation above 5%

	CPI	PME	Oils	Base Metals	CRSP 1-10
1973	8.78%	68.31%	10.04%	33.62%	-18.06%
1974	12.20%	-19.98%	-26.05%	-23.42%	-27.04%
1975	7.01%	-4.53%	23.64%	38.42%	38.75%
1977	6.77%	13.94%	-1.93%	-24.70%	-4.26%
1978	9.03%	0.33%	8.53%	12.95%	7.49%
1979	13.32%	128.35%	59.41%	72.96%	22.62%
1980	12.41%	67.97%	68.69%	44.63%	32.81%
1981	8.94%	-34.51%	-20.75%	-6.54%	-3.65%
1990	6.10%	-19.14%	-1.44%	-12.19%	-5.96%
Average	**9.40%**	**22.31%**	**13.35%**	**15.08%**	**4.75%**
Ann'd	**9.37%**	**12.92%**	**9.43%**	**10.58%**	**2.60%**
Real Ann'd	**N/A**	**3.25%**	**0.05%**	**1.11%**	**-6.19%**

Data source: Ken French Data Library, http://mba.tuck.dartmouth.edu/pages/faculty/ken.french/data_library.html.

So under appropriate circumstances, it might not be unreasonable to have an additional allocation to commodities producers. What might be those circumstances? Oil and base metals tend to be a boom-and-bust area. At some point in the future, the prices of their producing companies may fall out of favor, as they did during the mid-1980s, and their contribution to the market index may consequently fall. At such a time, they may warrant consideration in the portfolio. But probably not at present.

Finally, what about commodities futures exposure? It turns out that, like communism, they're great in theory, but don't pan out so well in practice. Before the 1990s, commodities futures had both high returns—higher even than stocks—and low correlations with both stocks and bonds. At about the same time, mean-variance-optimizers were becoming fashionable. When analysts fed these historical data into these engines, they naturally spat out "optimal" portfolios rich in commodities futures exposure. The ducks began to quack, and the investment industry began feeding them with a vengeance. By the mid-2000s, investors had their pick of managers and vehicles offering portfolios stuffed with commodities futures.

The problem with these is that enthusiasm for them derived from their high returns and low correlations to stocks and bonds in the pre-2000 era. Unfortunately, this world no longer exists. Back then, the major drivers in these markets were commodities producers for whom a fall in the price of their crude oil or corn output in the months or years it took to get those products to market might prove highly detrimental.

In this long-ago market where everyone wanted to sell commodities futures, buyers needed to be coaxed out of the woodwork by being offered a significant discount to the current spot price. Say a barrel of crude was selling for $20 per barrel in the 1990s. Only by selling a contract for $19 or less could a speculator be enticed to buy. Since the best estimate of the price of a commodity a year from now is today's price plus inflation, that $1 plus inflation discount offered the speculator enough of an expected return for him to bear the risk that the price would fall below $19, which looked like a pretty good bet in that era.

In that world, the speculator sold the producer an insurance policy against such a price fall. This phenomenon, in which the buyers of commodities futures earn an insurance premium, or "roll," is called "normal Keynesian backwardation," after the famous economist who first described the phenomenon in 1923. (Admittedly, backwardation is a somewhat simplified concept. Buyers of oil, such as airlines and trucking companies, also wish to hedge by taking the opposite side of the trade. But, in general, in most commodities markets, the hedging needs of the sellers overwhelm those of the consumers.)

Fast forward a quarter of a century. Now the biggest players are the likes of Pimco and Oppenheimer, who have sold the gullible on the pre-1990 record of commodities futures—never mind that prior to 1990 this strategy had been, for all practical purposes, non-investible. Now who's the buyer of insurance? Answer: the biggest, and most motivated, players—mutual fund companies, pension funds, and wealthy private accounts. And who are now the sellers? The producers, now in the fortunate position of being paid a positive roll on their short contracts. More important, what is being bought and sold by these behemoths? Answer: supposedly, protection against *inflation*, not deflation, as had been the case prior to 1990. When the financial service industry piled into these markets, they raised the price of the futures above the spot price. Thus, if the spot price didn't change—the most likely outcome—it produced a loss for the futures buyer when the contract matured—a condition known as "contango," which is manifest in the returns of commodities indexes and funds. [21]

By the turn of the new century, then, one of the major reasons to own commodities futures—the roll return—had reversed with a vengeance. The table below summarizes the returns of two commodities futures strategies versus simply owning the stocks of the producers themselves.

Index/Fund	Ann'd Return 2003–2012
PIMCO Commodity Real Return	7.70%
DJ-UBS Commodity Index	4.09%
Precious Metals Stocks	6.45%
Oil Stocks	13.57%
Base Metals Stocks	19.49%

Source data: Ken French database, Morningstar.com.

Figure 1-9 plots the value of a dollar invested in the spot index (that is, the prices of the commodities themselves) and the futures index since 2005. While the underlying (spot) prices of the commodities rose significantly, because of overcrowding/contango, the price of the index rose hardly at all. As a result, commodities fund investors who expected to benefit from increases in the prices of raw goods were sorely disappointed.

Clearly, you'd have been better off with a broad basket of the stocks of the commodities producers than with a commodities futures strategy. In the table above, I've chosen the Pimco fund because, in my opinion, it represents the best-case scenario—a top-performing actively managed commodities futures fund whose outperformance is unlikely to persist. The DJ-UBS index, on the other hand, represents a worst-case scenario, since it suffers somewhat from rolling its contracts on predictable dates, allowing arbitrageurs to "front run" them and thus reduce returns of the index. A good guess as to the "true return" available to investors is thus midway between the two values, probably closer to 6%.

Figure 1-9
Return of Commodities Futures/Spot

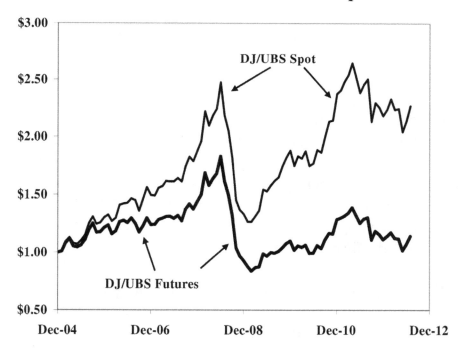

The other major "alternative" asset class is hedge funds, and the less said about them, the better. In addition to the overcrowding problem, they are also savaged by high fees. But since you're an investing adult, you're already smart enough to avoid them. And you'd be right. Over the past decade, you would have done just as well investing mainly in T-bills spiced with a soupçon of stocks, and at much lower cost.[22]

Bonds

Next, bonds. Between 1926 and 2012, the total nominal return for short Treasury bills was 3.53%; for 5-year Treasury notes, 5.34%; for long Treasuries, 5.70%; and for long corporate bonds, 6.09%.

First, observe that bills returned slightly more than inflation (2.98%) and that a decent premium (1.81%) was earned by extending Treasury maturities out to five years. But very little extra return was earned by extending maturities further or by lessening credit quality by buying high-grade corporate bonds.

At present, you're not going to be getting those returns going forward. Long-term nominal yields for T-bills, the 5-year intermediate Treasury, and the 30-year bond are, as of this writing, near zero, 1.5%, and less than 4%, respectively, thanks to the hyperaggressive stance of the Federal Reserve. Historical yields, by contrast, are much higher: 3%, 4%, and 5%, respectively, against which is placed a bogey of inflation that has historically averaged around 3%.

Worse, consider the historical best/worst rolling real annualized 10-year returns since 1926 for T-bills (+4.65%/-5.32%), 5-year Treasury notes (+9.40,/-4.44%,), and long government bonds (+11.93%/-6.49%). The problem, at present, is that the best-case scenario for the 5-year note and long bond has already been taken out by today's historically low yields, since the previously quoted maximum numbers for these two assets were the result of the precipitous fall from high yields in the 1980s. The +4.65% return for bills, on the other hand, was caused by the dramatic price deflation of the 1930s. A reprise of that scenario does not seem very likely either.

Consider the 5-year note, which as of this writing is yielding around 1.5% (having traded as low as 0.65% in 2013). With inflation running at around 2%, this corresponds to the -0.5% yield of the 5-year Treasury inflation protected security (TIPS). The most likely best-case scenario is that things stay more or less the same, which results in a negative real return in the vicinity of -0.5%. At the present moment, the only way of getting the Treasury note real return above sea level would be for inflation to fall even lower and remain so for some time, as occurred in the 1930s. This does not seem all that likely either.

On the other hand, the most likely worst-case scenario for bonds and notes would result merely from an increase in yields back to their historical levels, let alone the bloodbath that would result from even higher rates. If, for example, the yield on 5-year notes rose to 5%, this would result in a price fall of about 15% following on the heels of -0.5% real returns. I think the most likely 10-year expected real returns for nominal fixed-income asset classes at all maturities is half way between the most likely best-case scenario (no change in rates or inflation) and the most likely worst-case scenario (a slow return to historical yields), or around -1.5%.

Shades of Houston, we have a problem! The only way of getting even a paltry (as opposed to nearly zero) real return is by taking either the duration risk just documented or credit (default) risk, which is depicted in Figure 1-10, which plots the returns of two indexes of intermediate-term bonds: the Barcap Intermediate Treasury and Credit (corporate bond) series since December 31, 2007, the approximate beginning of the Global Financial Crisis.

This plot shows two things. First, corporates took a fairly substantial hit during the GFC. Second, they more than recovered from that tumble. In the long run, corporate bonds *do* have higher returns than Treasuries. Between March 1976 and March 2013, for example, the Barcap intermediate-term (4 to 5 years) corporate bond index returned 0.84% more than the analogous Treasury index. All's right with the world, you might say. Higher risk was repaid with higher return. But remember "Ilmanen risk": bad returns in bad times. You are most likely to need money for consumption or to buy cheap stocks right at the bottom of Figure 1-10.

Figure 1-10
Intermediate Corporates and Treasuries
after 2008

The same considerations apply to municipal bonds. The highest quality munis are equivalent to similarly rated corporates. During the GFC, they suffered about the same amount of damage as corporates: a few percent at the short end, up to 15% at the long end.

We'll wind up this chapter with a summary of the 10-year expected real returns of various asset classes, shown in Table 1-5.

Table 1-5. Expected Real Returns of Major Asset Classes over the Next 10 Years

Asset Class	Ten-Year Expected Real Return
U.S. Large-Cap Stocks	2%
U.S. Large-Value and Small-Cap Stocks	3%
U.S. Small-Value Stocks	4%
Developed Foreign Stocks	5%
Emerging Markets Stocks	4%
REITs	1%
Precious Metals Stocks	1%
Base Metals and Oil Stocks	3%
Bills, Notes, and Bonds	-1%

This table provides a good jumping off point for the next step in the process—the behavior of both theoretical and real-world portfolios.

CHAPTER 2

DIVERSIFY ME! PORTFOLIO MODELS: SIMPLE AND NOT SO SIMPLE

We'll start this chapter, as we did the last, with Uncle Fred's coin toss, which not only provides a simple and handy model for the behavior of stocks, but also helps us think about portfolio behavior. Instead of just one coin flip, we'll toss two coins simultaneously, yielding 4 possible outcomes:

Coin A	+30%	+30%	-10%	-10%
Coin B	+30%	-10%	+30%	-10%
50/50 A/B	+30%	+10%	+10%	-10%

Note that we now have more "moderate" results. In addition to the two extreme results of +30% and -10%, this exercise produces two additional intermediate results of +10%, which lower the SD of the "portfolio" to 14.14%.

Since you're an investing adult, you're good with numbers, and you immediately see that the SD has fallen by a factor of $\sqrt{2}$. If you play with this paradigm, you might fantasize that by increasing the number of coin flips, you'll decrease the SD of the portfolio by $\sqrt{n}$. By adding enough coin flips, you should be able to reduce the SD of the portfolio to near zero.

Even more tantalizing, the annualized return of the above series of 4 coin flips is 9.08%—nearly a full percentage point higher than the return of a single coin flip. Where does this extra return come from? It is the "rebalancing bonus" our coin-flip investor has made by reducing variance drag. Note that in the above example, the two coin flips are independent—that is, their correlation coefficient is zero. What if the correlation of the coin flips is -1.0? Then, since each heads for coin A yields a tail for coin B, and vice versa, the 50/50 return is +10% on each flip. So is the annualized return of the "portfolio." (Put another way, since the SD of the return is zero, so is the variance drag, so A = G.)

Let's play this paradigm out a little more by creating portfolios ranging from 100% A to 100% B. In Figure 2-1, I've plotted the returns and SDs of various mixtures of A and B. First, note that since the assets are identical, the 90/10 mix of A and B has the same return and SD as the 10/90 mix. Next, note that most of the diversification benefit occurs as one moves away from the 100/0 and 0/100 portfolios. By the point you reach, say, 70/30 or 30/70, most of the benefit in terms of both risk reduction and return enhancement has been obtained. In other words, there is relatively little daylight between the 70/30 and 30/70 portfolios and the "optimal" 50/50 one.

This observation is the most practical aspect of this simple paradigm. Once you've arrived at a prudent asset allocation, tweaking it in one direction or the other makes relatively little difference to your long-term results. Over the long run, your risk and return are governed mainly by your mix of risky and riskless assets: roughly, your stock/bond allocation. Beyond that, your allocation among different classes of risky assets—large, small, value, growth, foreign, domestic, and so forth—matters less than your ability to stick to it through thick and thin. Investing is a game won by the most disciplined, not by the smartest.

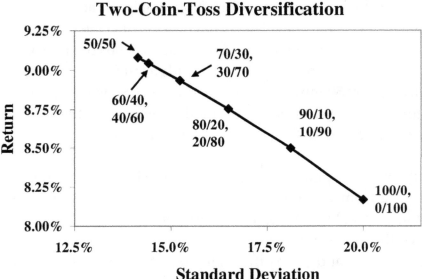

Figure 2-1
Two-Coin-Toss Diversification

Is it possible to find a large number of asset classes in the real world with near-zero correlations among all of them, and thus largely eliminate the risk from your portfolio? Of course not. There is no portfolio Santa Claus. In fact, most of the time you can't even find *two* risky asset classes with equivalent returns and a low correlation.

Here's why. Recall the above heuristic definition of risk: the probability of a loss in a bad state of the world—i.e., during a panic. A risky asset class, like the S&P 500 index of large company U.S. stocks, can lose more than 50% of its value. On one occasion (between September 1929 and June 1932), U.S. stocks lost nearly 90%. Almost by definition, these kinds of losses always occur in "bad states of the world."

Say we've discovered a second asset class with a zero correlation to the S&P. This characteristic makes it highly desirable, since it likely will have decent, or at least zero, returns when the S&P 500 tanks. This desirability bids up its price, thus reducing its future returns.

As discussed in the previous chapter, PME is a good example of this. These stocks do, in fact, have a very low correlation with U.S. large-cap stocks. Between 1964 and 2012, the correlation of the annual returns of the S&P 500 and an index of U.S. gold stocks (Ken French data series) was 0.153—as close to zero as you'll find in most circumstances.[1] For the 49 years between those two dates, the annualized returns and SDs of these two asset classes were as follows:

	Ann'd Return 1964–2012	Standard Deviation (Annual Returns)
S&P 500	9.56%	17.06%
Precious Metals Equity (PME)	6.95%	34.74%

(The sharp-eyed will notice that this example, using a 49-year period of calendar-year returns, is a different time period than the 50-year one mentioned in chapter 1 for PME, which began and ended in the middle of the calendar year. Moreover, the above table displays nominal returns, whereas the discussion of PME in the last chapter used real returns.) Over the long haul, because PME is a useful "noncorrelating asset class" that will mitigate loss during a bear market, it was highly desirable and thus had lower returns than the broad stock market, which is well represented by the S&P 500. Further, PME is considerably more risky than the S&P 500. (One final point: a zero correlation does not mean that this desirable behavior always shows up. During the GFC, PME saw even greater losses than the S&P 500.)

When we add PME to the S&P 500, just as in the two-coin-flip paradigm, return rises and risk falls, but only up to a point, and only slightly. Starting from the 100% S&P 500 end of the curve in the upper left corner of Figure 2-2, we see that addition of relatively small amounts of PME increases return and reduces risk a bit. But then things rapidly start to go downhill after more than 25% PME is added. Figure 2-3 magnifies the upper loop of Figure 2-2. This shows that adding up to 15% PME reduces risk, above which it rises. Portfolio return continues to rise with the addition of PME's portfolio composition to 25%, after which it, too, falls off rather rapidly.

The late Fisher Black, who won the Nobel Prize for his option pricing model, started out as a physicist; and Kenneth French, one of the great names in both empirical and theoretical finance, began as a mechanical engineer. If you belong to this group, and particularly if you're an engineer, it's all too easy to become entranced by the sort of backtesting exercise we've just done with the S&P 500 and PME. If only, you think, I could get another decade of data, and if only I could refine the numbers to one more decimal point, I will have achieved the Holy Grail of portfolio-dom.

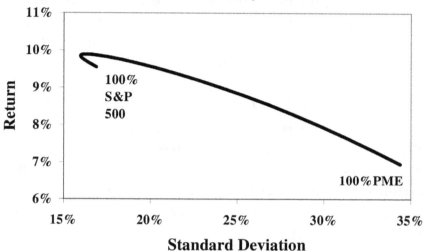

Figure 2-2
S&P 500/PME Mixes, 1964-2012

Figure 2-3
S&P 500/PME Mixes, 1964-2012

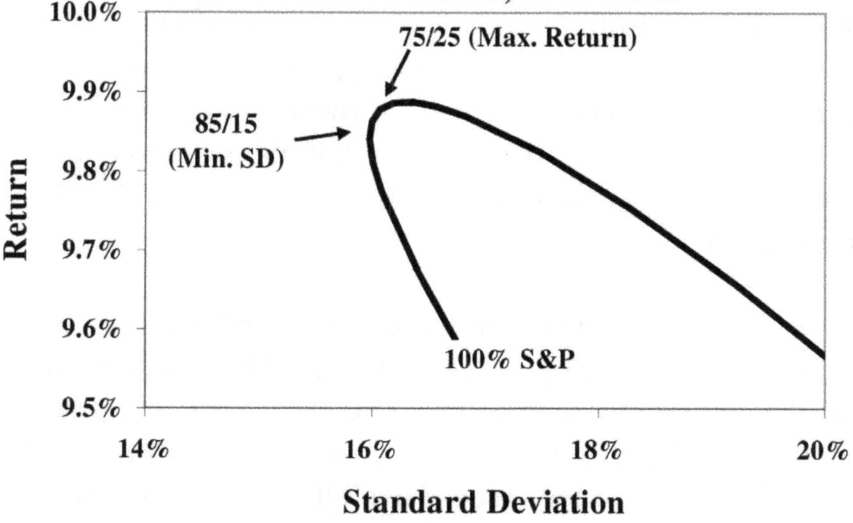

Beware! Financial systems are not airfoils or electrical circuits that respond identically, each and every time, to given inputs. Stock, bonds, and portfolios are different animals, and can behave unpredictably. You might conclude, for example, from the foregoing that adding a large helping of precious metals stocks to your portfolio is a good idea.

It might, or it might not. Consider, for example, what happens when I lower the return of the PME by 3% (to 3.95%) by subtracting a constant amount from each monthly return, the result of which I show in Figure 2-4. Note that while the 85/15 portfolio still minimizes risk, it does so at the cost of reducing return, and the 75/25 portfolio has a distinctly suboptimal risk/return trade-off.

This is not a theoretical exercise. When I wrote *The Intelligent Asset Allocator* in the late 1990s, investors couldn't give gold stocks away; anyone who recommended them in a portfolio was prone to being ridiculed. (I speak from personal experience.) By late 2011, with the dramatic recent rise in gold prices, they became an easier sell. Unfortunately, those who bought both PME and gold bullion were less happy with the dramatic price fall in both that occurred in 2013. Still, if you want to add up to several percent to your portfolio, be my guest. But 15%, 25%, or more? Then you're taking real risk.

This exercise also tells us something else: if the long-term returns of the asset classes in your portfolio are different enough, the "rebalancing bonus" can be negative. As we see in Figure 2-4, by tweaking the PME return lower, adding even a little bit of it to a broad market index reduced overall portfolio returns. In the real world, this occasionally happens even without tweaking results. For example, in the 20 years between 1990 and 2009, the S&P 500 returned 8.21% annually, and large Japanese stocks *lost* 2.27% annually. You'd have been better off simply letting your U.S. and Japanese stocks take their long rides up and down, respectively, without rebalancing. A portfolio that started out at 50/50 returned 5.16% if not rebalanced. If rebalanced annually, it earned 3.64% as U.S. stocks were sold each year and tossed down the Nikkei drain.

Figure 2-4
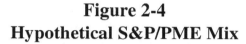
Hypothetical S&P/PME Mix

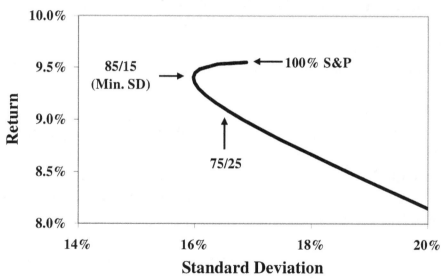

Generally, however, in the very long term, national equity markets tend to have similar risk premiums. For example, if we extend our analysis of Japanese and U.S. stocks back to 1970, we find that over the ensuing 40 years (1970–2009) they had similar returns (9.38% and 9.87%, respectively), and so rebalancing did produce a positive bonus. In a sense, the rebalancing bonus among stock asset classes can be viewed as a kind of risk premium for betting that stock asset classes will revert to the mean and produce similar long-run returns. This brings up an interesting, and not entirely theoretical, point. In a truly efficient, random-walk world (in the argot of finance, "i.i.d.," that is, "independent and identically distributed"), there obviously should be no rebalancing bonus, since the decision to rebalance implies that lower/higher past returns relative to other asset classes imply higher/lower future ones—in other words, that asset-class returns tend to revert to the mean.

Is this actually true? Unfortunately, it's almost impossible to prove mean reversion for any individual asset class, because we are interested mainly in relatively long periods, on the order of 5 to 10 years. Shiller's series, mentioned earlier, extends back just 142 years, so there are only 28 and 14 nonoverlapping 5- and 10-year periods, respectively, which are insufficient to resolve the question.

When academics aggregate stock return data from many nations, statistically significant evidence of mean reversion appears. But since all the data come from the same time period, it's hard to tell.[2] (Or as Paul Samuelson is said to have lamented, "We only have two hundred years of data.")

In the very long run, of course, stocks have significantly higher returns than bonds, and so return is "lost" by periodically rebalancing between stocks and bonds. To use an extreme (and highly unrealistic) example, if a 50/50 portfolio of the S&P 500 and 5-year notes was formed on December 31, 1925 and left undisturbed, by December 31, 2012 it would have consisted of 97.5% stocks and returned 9.01%. Had it been rebalanced back to 50/50 at the end of each year, it would have returned 8.14%—almost a full percent per year less.

To generalize: Over very long periods, a stock/bond portfolio, if not rebalanced, will become top-heavy with stocks. The unrebalanced portfolio is "better" only in the sense that it has higher return, which came at the cost of much higher risk in the later years. This nicely makes the point that the real purpose of rebalancing is to reduce risk and that in the very long run this will obviously reduce return. Since the essence of an investment strategy is to select the appropriate tradeoff between risk and return, the decision *not* to rebalance a portfolio will most often, in the long run, constitute an active decision to increase both its risk and its expected return.

No Free Lunch: A VXXing Problem

Thanks to the genius of the financial services industry, there are now products at the extreme edge of noncorrelating risky assets that are based on futures contracts for stock indexes and volatility indexes that have a very high negative correlation with stocks. A particularly popular one is the VXX, an ETF that tracks volatility futures indexes contracts. When the markets are particularly rocky, it will have strong positive returns and, during those brief periods, will save a lot of your bacon.

To examine the use of this vehicle, which has only a very short history, I chose the 2 years from 2010 to 2011. This was a period of historically reasonable stock performance, during which the S&P 500 returned an annualized 8.39%. In that same period, the correlation of monthly returns and the VXX with the S&P 500 was, hold onto your hat, -0.79. This negative correlation did not come without a price: an annualized return of -48.9%. That is to say, during the 2-year period, a dollar invested in the S&P 500 grew to $1.17, while a dollar invested in VXX fell to $0.26.

Figure 2-5 shows what would have happened if you had mixed the two asset classes. Yes, adding a small amount of VXX *did* reduce portfolio volatility, but it also gutted returns. By contrast, simply mixing the S&P 500 with T-bills, which had a near-zero return during the period, was a much better bet.

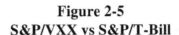

Figure 2-5
S&P/VXX vs S&P/T-Bill

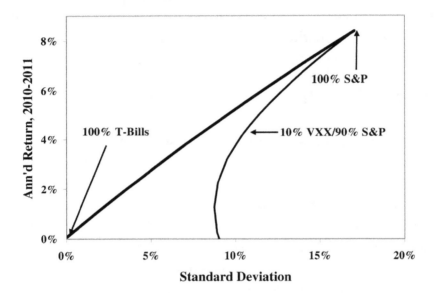

I hope by now I've convinced you that there are no free volatility-reducing lunches that will inexpensively reduce your portfolio risk, and there is no risk fairy to insure the risky parts of your portfolio on the cheap. Yes, there are people who—and vehicles that—will do this for you, but they will cost you a pretty penny. If you want to reduce your portfolio risk, it is far more efficient to simply substitute riskless assets for risky ones rather than try to inoculate your risky assets with other risky and noncorrelating ones.

On the Frontier

Let's make the process more complicated by using several components. Figure 2-6 plots random portfolios consisting of several different asset classes over a given time period. It doesn't matter what they are, nor does it matter what time period we're looking at. The underlying principle we're trying to illustrate remains the same. (Well, OK, since you're curious, the asset classes are the S&P 500, U.S. small stocks, the EAFE Europe, Japan, and Pacific Rim indexes, the Morningstar Precious Metals fund average, and 5-year Treasury notes, between 1990 and 1996, rebalanced annually.)

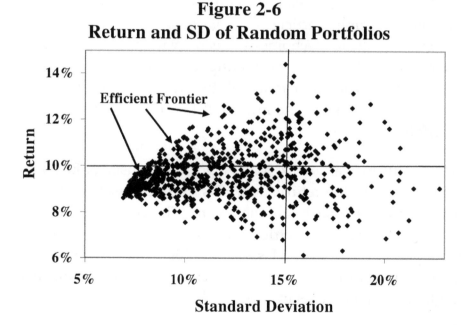

Figure 2-6
Return and SD of Random Portfolios

I've drawn 2 axis lines within the graph. The first is a vertical one at 15% of risk. Imagine yourself traveling up this line. If you've decided that you can tolerate this high risk level, you want to get as much return as you can for it, that is, you want to go as far up the line as you can.

Conversely, consider all the portfolios lying on the horizontal axis, which corresponds to all the portfolios that return 10% per year. Obviously, you want to go as far to the left of this line as you can, getting that 10% of return for the least amount of risk.

Note how sharply defined the "northwest" edge of the plot is. Those portfolios yield the highest return for a given amount of risk or the least risk for a given amount of return. These favored portfolios are the so-called "efficient frontier" of portfolio construction.

In 1952, a young economics Ph.D. named Harry Markowitz published a seminal article in the *Journal of Finance* that described a mathematical technique—mean variance optimization (hereafter, MVO)—for calculating the composition of these maximally efficient portfolios, all the way from the "minimum variance" portfolio at the lower left to the "maximum return" portfolio at the top.[3]

The inputs to Markowitz' MVO algorithm consist of just 3 sets of parameters: the returns and SDs for each asset, along with the correlation matrix among them. (The returns used must be *arithmetic*, not geometric, since the MVO algorithm already "punishes" those asset classes with high SD/variance. Using geometric returns would double-count the disadvantage of high-SD/variance asset classes.)

Table 2-1 displays a simple, and highly illustrative, "Markowitz Grid" for the annual returns for three asset classes for 1972–1990: the S&P 500, a long government bond index, and the Goldman Sachs Commodities Futures Index (GSCI).

Table 2-1. Markowitz Grid and Its MVO Outputs

Panel A. The Markowitz Grid for a simple three-asset portfolio.

	Return	SD	S&P 500	Long Gov't	GSCI
S&P 500	10.99%	17.50%	1.00		
Long Gov't	8.48%	12.38%	0.40	1.00	
GSCI	16.26%	23.52%	-0.37	-0.28	1.00

Panel B. Outputs from the above Inputs (Corner Portfolios).

	Return	SD	S&P 500	Long Gov't	GSCI
Corner 1 (minimum variance)	11.19%	8.59%	23.67%	49.22%	27.12%
Corner 2	13.72%	11.19%	48.12%	0.00%	51.88%
Corner 3 (maximum return)	16.26%	23.52%	0.00%	0.00%	100.00%

Source: Computations from MvoPlus, Efficient Solutions, effisols.com.

What could be easier? Simply collect the returns, SDs, and correlations for your asset classes, then pour them into the magic black box (in my case, MvoPlus from Efficient Solutions). Out pop the high-returning, low-volatility "corner" portfolios, a set of defined allocations strung out along the efficient frontier. (One interpolates between pairs of adjacent corner portfolios to obtain more refined allocations; for example, the portfolio half way between corners 1 and 2 consists of 35.90% S&P 500, 24.60% Long Governments, and 39.50% GSCI.)

I suggest a more profitable way to design your portfolio: stuff half the money in your mattress and lend the other half to your drug-addled nephew. The problem with MVO is twofold. First, its outputs are highly sensitive to its inputs, particularly asset return. Increase an asset's return by a few percent, and it dominates the portfolio. Lower it by a few percentage points, and it disappears entirely. Second, and more important, because of the tendency of asset classes to mean revert, your optimizer is likely to overexpose you to assets that have had high prior returns, and consequently have low returns going forward. (Wags sometimes refer to the mean variance optimizer as an "error maximizer.")

I picked the above 3 assets and the 1972–1990 time period in Table 2-1 for a specific reason. In the early 1990s, MVOs began to appear on analysts' desktop PCs, yielding the commodities-heavy portfolios displayed in the table. In the previous chapter, I described how the "financialization" of commodities futures dramatically changed the nature of this asset class and lowered future returns. Financialization had another adverse consequence for commodities futures: it increased its correlation with other risky assets. When a risky asset can be bought or sold with the push of a button (as a commodities futures mutual fund now can) during a panic, investors will hit that sell button along with those of all of their other risky assets.

In *The Intelligent Asset Allocator* I conducted an exercise that demonstrated just how dangerous optimizers can be. I began with the same 6 stock asset classes displayed in Figure 2-6 (S&P 500, U.S. small, European, Japanese, Pacific Rim, and gold stocks). I found that optimizing the portfolio every five years based on the prior period's 5-year returns produced an overall return that was 7.39% *worse* than what resulted simply through the use of a naïve equal mix of all 6 asset classes.

How, then, to design a portfolio? By answering a series of questions, in the following sequence, and in decreasing order of importance:

- What overall mix of risky and riskless assets (roughly, stocks versus bonds/cash) do I want?
- How much of my risky assets do I invest in the U.S., developed foreign markets, and emerging markets?
- How much tilt do I want towards value stocks, small stocks, and other, newer returns factors, such as momentum and profitability?
- How much exposure do I want to "ancillary asset classes," such as REITs, PME, and NR stocks?

Step 1: The Stock/Bond Mix

Your stock/bond mix depends upon several factors, the three most important of which are your *tolerance of* risk, your *capacity for* risk, and your *need for* risk.

We'll spend most of chapter 4 covering how your stock/bond mix should vary over the life cycle, but for now I'll offer some introductory comments. All three factors—tolerance of risk, capacity for risk, and need for risk—must be considered jointly. To demonstrate the process, let's start with a 65-year-old retiree, Sadie, who has a $1,000,000 portfolio and $40,000 in living expenses, but no Social Security or pension.

The primary goal of retirement savings is to completely and safely cover basic living expenses over the rest of the investor's lifetime, which we'll discuss in much greater detail in chapter 4. For now, assume that this amount consists of 25 years of residual living expenses (RLE—the amount a retiree needs to live on after the receipt of Social Security, pension, and other periodic benefits). Since Sadie barely has this, she has zero *capacity* for risk. Every 4% loss in her portfolio theoretically makes her destitute for one year of her remaining life. That is, she cannot afford to lose any of her nest egg in stocks, so her entire portfolio should be invested in low-risk assets whose payoff time scale profile matches her retirement needs: TIPS, plain-vanilla Treasuries, single-premium fixed annuities, CDs, and perhaps some short- or intermediate-term corporates and municipal bonds.

The key word in the previous sentence is "matches." An inflation-adjusted annuity yielding her annual RLE precisely matches those liabilities; so, too, does a long enough TIPS ladder with annual maturities in the amount of her RLE (were that possible, which it isn't). Both the inflation-adjusted annuity and TIPS ladder constitute a "liability matching portfolio" (LMP). A traditional 60/40 portfolio most certainly does not. In *The Ages of the Investor*, I covered in some detail the pros and cons of both commercial annuities and TIPS ladders in detail. Suffice it to say that neither is perfect. With a commercial annuity you're taking considerable credit (default) risk, whereas with a TIPS ladder you run the risk of outliving it.[4]

Additionally, Sadie has no *need* to take risk, since she has already acquired precisely enough assets on which to retire. Her risk tolerance is irrelevant, since her capacity for and need for risk already control her asset allocation.

Now, let's magically give Sadie pension and Social Security income equal to her living expenses. Her *capacity* for risk has now increased dramatically. Since she no longer needs her nest egg to live on, she's in reality managing it for her heirs and her charitable interests. Thus, her allocation is now determined by her *tolerance* for risk. Aside from an adequate emergency fund (preferably in a taxable account), if she can sleep through the sort of market decline seen during the Great Depression or the GFC, there's no reason she couldn't invest all of her portfolio in risky assets.

To complete the tolerance-capacity-need risk paradigm: the investor whose retirement income requirements cannot be met by investing in safe assets *needs* to take risk (pretty much everyone early in his or her life cycle does). Only after an adequate nest egg has been built up—with luck, before retirement—does the need to take risk disappear.

The same would be true, I might add, if Sadie had no Social Security or pension income but instead had a $5,000,000 portfolio. In this case, her stock portfolio would yield her $100,000 per year in income, which is more than adequate to meet her needs and provide her with a good margin of safety. If, as in the Great Depression, dividends fell by half (versus a nearly 90% price fall), she could still safely spend 1%, or half of today's 2% yield. During the GFC, real dividends fell by just 23%, and then only briefly. Again, in this felicitous circumstance, it's Sadie's *tolerance* for risk that controls her asset allocation.

Now let's take Sadie's niece Sally, who's just started work as a freelance editor, with no pension plan. Sally's a downshifter who figures she'll need about $30,000 to live on in retirement, which is $15,000 more than her projected Social Security benefit. She thinks she can save $4,000 per year.

As we'll see in chapter 4, there is almost no way she'll be able to retire much before age 75 unless she invests aggressively — that is, she has a high *need* to take risk. Additionally, she'll need a high *tolerance* for risk. If she does not have that, she's in a real bind. Even more unfortunate, she has, in reality, almost no *capacity* for risk, since there is little margin for error in her investment trajectory. Sally's dire situation is emblematic of that of the vast majority of American workers: a high need for risk, no capacity for it, and probably inadequate risk tolerance to boot. Her best shot at a decent retirement resides in her aunt's will.

Recall that Sadie's LMP of safe bonds was 25 times her RLE, so each year she'll spend about 4% of that safe nest egg. We also determined that she could safely spend 1% per year (half the current 2% yield) of her stocks. This suggests, then, a formula for safe retirement spending: stocks/100 + bonds/25. For example, a portfolio of $500,000 stocks and $250,000 bonds yields a safe withdrawal of $15,000 per year ($500,000/100 + $250,000/25).

The average investor is most constrained by his or her *tolerance* for risk. A classic study by economist Robert B. Barsky and his colleagues asked subjects the following question:

> Suppose that you are the only income earner in the family, and you have a good job guaranteed to give you your current (family) income every year for life. You are given the opportunity to take a new and equally good job, with a 50-50 chance that it will double your (family) income and a 50-50 chance that it will cut your (family) income by a third. Would you take the new job?[5]

This sort of question yields the so-called "relative risk aversion" (RRA), which, roughly translates as how frightened you are of risk. For example, if you answered "yes" to the above question, your RRA was less than 2. If you answered "no," it was more than 2. If you answered "not sure," it was close to 2. In this special case, RRA is approximated as [(1-x)/x], so if you were at equipoise with a small 10% loss of salary, your RRA zooms up to 9. Contrariwise, if you're willing to suffer a 50% chance of a 100% loss of salary, your RRA is zero. (The RRA only makes sense as long as the expected return of the bet is not less than zero.)

Barsky et al. found that for most people, the RRA measured from sequential questions of this sort was quite high. Nearly two thirds of the respondents would not accept even a 50/50 chance of a twenty percent loss of income, which means that their RRA was greater than 4. The researchers also found that the RRA correlated not only with the percent of equity held by respondents, as might be expected, but also with other risk-taking behavior. Those who smoked, drank heavily, or did not buy insurance all had lower RRAs.[6]

Mind you, these data refer exclusively to how much risk people *say* they can tolerate—again, think flight simulator versus an actual crash. Let's start by looking in Table 2-2 at what the 2008–2009 bear market did to actual asset classes, from the top in October 2007 to the bottom in early March 2009.

First, notice that there was no place to hide. Next, notice how exposure to the small and value risk premiums exposed the true nature of those risks, with losses higher than of the broad market. Even investors who thought they had a conservative allocation, in the range of 50/50, lost nearly a third of their nest egg and, along with it, their nerve.

Table 2-2. Peak to Trough (Defined as October 9, 2007-March 6, 2009) for Various Risky Asset Classes

Asset Class	Total Return 10/31/2007-3/6/2009
U.S. Large Market (VFIAX)	-54.7%
U.S. Large Value (DFLVX)	-62.8%
U.S. Small Market (DFSCX)	-61.4%
U.S. Small Value (DFSVX)	-63.2%
REITs (VGSLX)	-70.3%
Precious Metals Equity (GDX)*	-30.0%
Developed International Large Market (VTMGX)	-58.8%
Developed International Large Value (DFIVX)	-64.8%
Developed International Small Market (DFISX)	-58.4%
Developed International Small Value (DISVX)	-58.6%
Developed Markets REITs (DFITX)	-71.8%
Emerging Markets Large Market (DFEMX)	-58.2%
Emerging Markets Large Value (DFEVX)	-63.4%
Emerging Markets Small Market (DEMSX)	-62.9%

Data source: finance yahoo.com historical adjusted prices.
*GDX sustained healthy gains during the initial phase of the crisis, but between 7/14/08 and 10/23/2008 it suffered a 65.8% loss of total return.

In 2009, veteran *Wall Street Journal* reporter Neal Templin wrote a *cri de coeur* entitled "Honey, I Shrunk the Nest Egg (And I'm Sorry)," in which he described how he had overestimated his risk tolerance:

My company retirement accounts, despite what
I thought was a relatively conservative mix, were
down close to 35% in early March from the fall of
2007. That, in turn, forced me to do some painful
thinking about how much risk I can stomach on
my family's behalf, and how much money we
can expect to have in retirement. My conclusion:
My longtime portfolio allocation of 50% stocks
and 50% bonds wasn't safe enough.[7]

Readers of this book fall into two groups: those who invested
through the GFC and those who didn't. If you did, then you,
like Mr. Templin, have a pretty good idea of your true risk
tolerance and thus what your stock/bond allocation should be.
You probably have also tailored your portfolio accordingly.

If you began your investing journey after 2009 or haven't yet
started, then you're an investment virgin. It's safest to assume
that your true capacity is low, and you should start with a
conservative stock/bond allocation, say in the range of 50/50. If,
like Mr. Templin, you find that you have a lower risk tolerance
than you thought, at least you'll discover it relatively early and
with a relatively small portfolio.

Step 2: Broad Stock Asset Classes

Deployment among stock asset classes is relatively easier. The
obvious place to start is with the total world stock market, as
mirrored reasonably well by the FTSE Global All Cap Index,
which in early 2014 was split 48/52 between U.S. and foreign
equities. From there, we make three adjustments to the foreign
allocation, two down and one up. First, the downs: if you're like

most people, your retirement liabilities will be in dollars, so a 52% foreign allocation is inappropriately high. Second, foreign stocks not only are slightly more difficult and expensive to trade but also are subject to foreign tax withholding. This presents no problem in taxable accounts, since those taxes will offset your liability to the IRS, but you lose that deduction if you hold foreign stocks in a sheltered account. This doesn't mean that you shouldn't own them at all in an IRA or 401(k), it's merely a thumb on the domestic side of the scale. The up adjustment is a temporary one, since foreign stocks, as was discussed in chapter 1, currently have higher expected returns. So at the time of this writing, a foreign stock allocation somewhere in the 30% to 45% region seems reasonable.

There are many ways to skin the stock allocation cat. As a first approximation, there's nothing wrong with using only two stock funds: the Vanguard Total Stock Market Fund for the U.S. portion and the Vanguard Total International Stock Index Fund. These two funds expose you to virtually all of the world's publicly traded stocks that have even a modest market cap.

Step 3: How Much Tilt? What Kind of Tilt?

In chapter 1, we discussed how small and value stocks had higher expected returns than the broad market. Later on we'll see how aggressive periodic investing early in the life cycle is much less risky than it looks. That doesn't mean, however, that the lack of risk tolerance in younger investors won't emotionally derail the majority of them.

The first question, already addressed in chapter 1, is whether tilting towards small and value stocks still carries a premium.

The answer, I think, is still yes. The premium for small stocks is a classic example of Ilmanen Risk: bad returns in bad times, which certainly showed up in the two great panics of the last hundred years: the 1929–1932 and 2008–2009 bear markets. Ditto for value exposure, plus the behavioral attraction of investors towards growth stocks, also discussed in chapter 1.

Some worry that since large institutional funds—particularly hedge funds and ETFs—are now chasing these factors, these premiums will erode or completely disappear. This may now be true in normal times, but in bad states of the world, to paraphrase Billy Ray Valentine in *Trading Places*, the suckers will get cleared out—not just naïve small investors but also hedge funds, which will be forced to unload their positions as their clients pull out and their liquidity—that is, their sources of leverage—dries up faster than a rain gully in the desert. This will likely produce, as happened in 2008–2009, a sharp contraction in prices that will remind investors of the risk of the value and small premiums, and so set the stage for subsequent higher returns.

Theoretically, the young saver should tilt her portfolio heavily towards small value stocks. In *The Ages of the Investor* I examined the process of dollar-cost averaging, as a young saver might, into the S&P 500 and Fama-French small value series over a series of rolling 30-year periods. The value premium, for example, is quite fickle. Since 1926, it has yielded negative returns for as long as 15 years. The small premium is even worse, yielding negative returns for as long as 30 years.

This occasional long-lasting underperformance of both the small and value factors, though, is of more concern to lump-sum investments than to those with a stream of periodic investments, since having the ability to occasionally purchase small and value stocks at low prices mitigates any temporary underperformance of small and value stocks.

In *The Ages of the Investor*, I analyzed the tilt towards small and value with the following paradigm. I began with the inflation-adjusted return for the longest data series we have for small-value stocks — the Fama-French small-value index, with utilities included, between July 1926 and October 2011. This index returned 10.50% real-annualized, which was 3.88% per year more than the 6.62% real-annualized return for the S&P 500.

Figure 2-7
Nest Egg: SV = S&P 500 Return

Now imagine that a real $100 per month (in 1926 dollars) was invested for 30 years — 360 monthly purchases — for all of the starting dates between July 1926 and November 1981. In each and every case, the small-value strategy beats investing in the S&P 500 — sometimes by a huge margin.

But the 3.88% annualized return advantage of small value stocks during this period is unrealistic, as already discussed. Figure 2-7 demonstrates that when the returns of small value stocks and the S&P were equalized at 6.62% by adjusting the monthly returns down by a constant amount, the small value strategy still won 71% of the time because the greater volatility of small-value stocks allowed for a greater number of shares to be bought at lower prices.

Figure 2-8
Success Rates of Small Value vs S&P 500

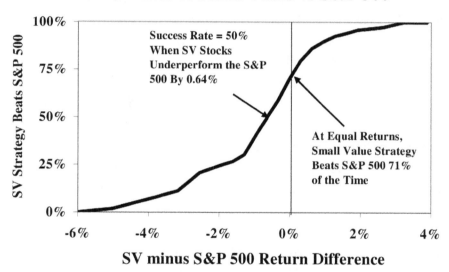

SV minus S&P 500 Return Difference

The reason, once again, is the paradoxical nature of the small-value strategy: higher volatility than a conventional 100% S&P 500 strategy and, thus, more opportunity to buy at much lower prices. The excess returns of both strategies, of course, come with a cost. Small value stocks have much greater volatility and, thus, far greater emotional demands on the investor—in plain English, uncertainty that will have your stomach doing back flips. (Later on, we'll discuss leveraging stock exposure, another strategy that also sports the paradoxical phenomenon of higher returns through higher volatility early in the savings phase.)

Nonetheless, discipline does have its rewards. Figure 2-8 plots what happens to the success rate of the small value strategy versus the S&P strategy as a function of the returns difference between the two asset classes; not until small value stocks underperform the S&P 500 by 0.64% is the 50% success point breached.

During the past decade, two additional "tilt factors" have emerged: momentum and profitability. First, momentum. It has long been known that shares with high past short-term returns tend to have higher short-term future returns. Between January 1927 and March 2013, for example, a portfolio of high-momentum stocks has beaten a portfolio of low-momentum (that is, negative returning) stocks by 6.91% per year. Recently, strategies that harvest these returns have become quite popular with hedge funds. Figure 2-9 plots the 10-year annualized return of the momentum factor (MOM: high momentum stocks versus low momentum stocks).

Note, first of all, how MOM was strongly negative during the worst periods of economic crisis. In actuality, these two "momentum crashes" occurred just *after* the stock market rebounded in July 1932 and March 2009. Figures 2-10 and 2-11 demonstrate this curious relationship between the returns to the market, value, and momentum factors around the time of the market bottoms in mid-1932 and early 2009.

Figure 2-9
10-Year Trailing Return Momentum Factor

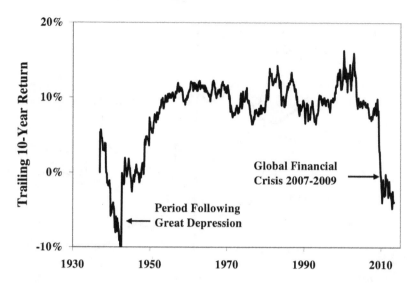

Figure 2-10
Returns Factors around July 1932 Bottom

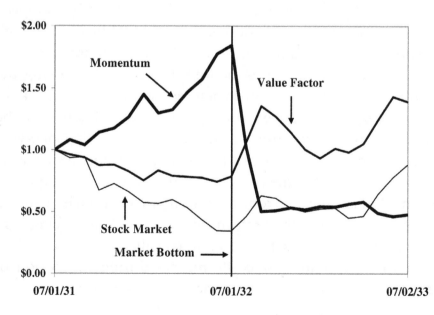

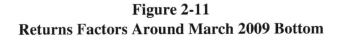

Figure 2-11
Returns Factors Around March 2009 Bottom

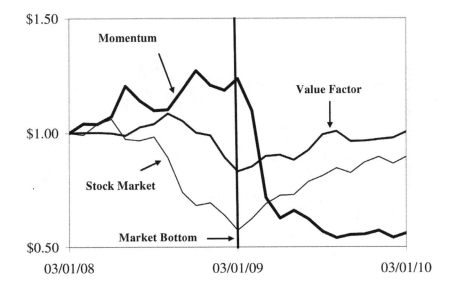

While many do not consider momentum to be a risk premium, these two plots suggest that it very well may be. What happens during a severe market downturn is that blue-chip, "high quality" companies suffer less damage. In the months leading up to a cataclysmic market bottom, these wind up being the high-momentum stocks. But when the market snaps back after the recovery, as happened after July 1932 and March 2009, the "junkier" low-momentum stocks with poor trailing one-year returns recover most strongly, producing a "momentum crash." The key thing is that the overall return of momentum exposure during the bad times surrounding the market bottom is negative, a classic example of "bad returns in bad times," qualifying it, in my opinion, as a risk factor. Paradoxically, it is an excellent short-term diversifier, since its returns during the period of worst returns—the first year in each plot—is positive.[8]

Finally, recent research demonstrates that firms with high profitability, which we can define here as the earnings/book value ratio, tend to also earn a premium, in the range of several percent per year. This is surprising, since these tend to be growth companies.[9]

To sum up, we've identified four "tilt factors" that generate excess returns: small size, value, momentum, and profitability. The small premium is tiny, at most a percent or two, whereas the other three are in the range of several percent. At first blush, this all seems too good to be true: added up, the total "tilt premium" appears to be in the vicinity of 15% to 20% per year

Not so fast. First, since all of these factors are long/short portfolios, the long-only investor gets just half of these. Next, depending on the way the market is sorted on these two factors, the small value corner of the investment universe consists of several percent of total market cap at best. Add sorts for momentum and profitability, and you're down to a poorly diversified fraction of a percent of the investable universe. In the real world, the best you can do is to try to find reasonably diversified portfolios consisting of a large, representative sample of the market that score reasonably well on a weighted scale of all the factors, which drastically cuts the overall expected benefit from grazing multiple premiums— and that's before factoring in the rapidly escalating amount of money chasing these strategies. As I write this, mutual fund and ETF providers are already rolling out products that capture various combinations of these factors, but because of this multiple-factor size constraint, none will be able to load strongly on all of them; optimal strategies will likely involve relatively weak sorts on multiple factors and offer at best a few percent return premium over the broad market.

Moreover, researchers will, in the future, identify yet more factors associated with excess returns, so this is a highly fluid area. You should stay tuned, and caution is advised.

Step 4: Ancillary Stock Asset Classes

I suspect that if you're reading this book, you're looking for something a bit more complex than the average portfolio. First, it's worth breaking the foreign stock allocation down into developed markets and emerging markets. You can even, if you like, further divide an untilted developed markets portfolio into European, Japanese, and Pacific Rim components. Second, I think that a small contribution to REITs is worthwhile, taking into consideration whether or not the U.S. and international stock index funds in your portfolio already own them. For example, Vanguard's broad-based index funds include REITs, while the broadly diversified funds offered by Dimensional Fund Advisors don't. Last, a smidgen of precious metals and resource stocks—beyond those already held in your main foreign and domestic fund holdings—is likely worthwhile as a bulwark against inflation, which financial history shows to be the most salient macroeconomic risk facing the investor in a fiat money world. To summarize, your stock holdings should be divided among these broad asset-class categories, in roughly descending order of priority:

- U.S. equities
- Developed nations foreign equities
- Emerging markets equities
- Precious metals stocks
- Oil and base metals producing stocks

Happiness Is a Warm Bond

Bonds are easier. As discussed earlier in the chapter, they're your lifeboat and your opportunity supply—an option on the future, if you will. As we saw in Figure 1-10, in bad times corporate bonds can take a real haircut (as can longer munis) to pay your living expenses. During the last few bear markets, longer Treasuries did very well. But beware. Sooner or later, we're going to have an inflationary crisis, and in such an environment, long duration will be a killer. Stick to short Treasuries, CDs, and munis. For the first two, I'd own them individually—a 5-year ladder, with an average maturity of around 2.5 years, is the furthest out I'd go. Because of the opacity and spreads and the need for wide diversification in the municipal bond market, the best choices, by far, are the Vanguard municipal bond funds, going out no further than their "intermediate" national and state-level funds. One word of warning about state-specific funds is in order. Although it's tempting to avoid state income tax with these, I'd make such a fund no more than half of your muni holdings because of the systematic risk of state-level fiscal problems.

Except in extraordinary circumstances, I don't like corporate bonds. Besides their stock-like behavior in a panic, there's also a good theoretical reason not to hold them, which is the agency conflict between a company's bondholders and its stockholders. Since bondholders have no upside beyond par at maturity, they rationally care only about the safety of interest and principal coverage. Stockholders, in contrast, care at least as much about the potentially unlimited upside potential of equity and are thus rationally willing to seek out risk to get that upside. The problem is that it's the stockholders who get to vote, not the bondholders.

If share prices fall by half or more, you're going to be selling a fair amount of fixed-income instruments to make stock purchases at low prices. How will you feel about burning your newly desirable cash during such a downturn, after you've already plowed a fair amount of your liquid reserves into risky equities? More important, how much of your discipline will remain? You won't know the answers to those questions until this actually happens, but if your "cash" holdings are not of the highest quality, and possibly of short duration as well, it won't matter.

Market Efficiency and Dynamic Asset Allocation

In 2009, the venerable Jeremy Grantham, cofounder of the Grantham Mayo van Otterloo asset-management firm, opined to Joe Nocera in the pages of *The New York Times*:

> The incredibly inaccurate efficient market theory was believed in totality by many of our financial leaders, and believed in part by almost all. It left our economic and government establishment sitting by confidently, even as a lethally dangerous combination of asset bubbles, lax controls, pernicious incentives and wickedly complicated instruments led to our current plight. "Surely, none of this could be happening in a rational, efficient world," they seemed to be thinking. And the absolutely worst part of this belief set was that it led to a chronic underestimation of the dangers of asset bubbles breaking.[10]

Many share Mr. Grantham's frustration. How could supposedly "efficient" markets have led to the disastrous tech bubble of the late 1990s or the more recent GFC?

The problem, I think, arises from the impracticality of the rigorous definitions of the EMH's three forms: weak (future price changes cannot be predicted from prior changes), semistrong (price changes cannot be predicted by existing publicly available information), and strong (price changes cannot be predicted either from existing public or *nonpublic* information).

In a letter to Robert Shiller, Paul Samuelson helped resolve this problem by describing two different forms of market efficiency: "microefficiency," meaning the inability to generate excess risk-adjusted returns through security selection, and "macroefficiency," by which he meant the degree to which the overall market valuation corresponded to its intrinsic value. "Samuelson's Dictum," Shiller wrote, was that markets were microefficient, but macroinefficient.[11]

In other words, Samuelson intuitively understood what all investing adults now know: that it's nearly impossible to identify persistently successful stock and bond pickers, and those who do achieve high returns almost always revert to the mean going forward. But Samuelson also believed (as do Robert Shiller and this author) that from time to time the markets go barking mad, as they clearly did in the late 1990s.

The best, and certainly the most detailed, practical formulation of market efficiency is finance academic Meir Statman's.[12] He posits that markets can be:

- Unbeatable: it is impossible to consistently earn excess risk-adjusted returns in the market through security selection. This corresponds to Samuelson's "microefficiency."
- Rational: the overall price level of the market always reflects reasonable economic expectations. This corresponds to Samuelson's "macroefficiency."
- Random: this corresponds exactly to classical weak-form efficiency.
- Economically efficient: markets always achieve economically optimal results, either at the microeconomic or macroeconomic level. This corresponds to Mr. Grantham's assignment of the role played by supposedly efficient markets in the GFC.
- Fair: markets are always judicially and morally fair. This tends to be a political canard.

We'll dispose of the last three quickly, and in reverse order. The societal fairness of markets is such a laughable concept that it needs no further discussion. Regarding economic efficiency, even the staunchest of libertarians will concede that some regulation and legal oversight of contract enforcement and criminal prosecution of fraud, and even of reasonable reserve requirements (the absence of which was a major contributor to the GFC) are necessary. Randomness, too, fell by the wayside long ago. Almost as soon as Eugene Fama wrote his papers on market efficiency, he and others described the momentum anomaly. Numerous other anomalies have since been found.

We are left, then, with unbeatability and rationality. You're an investing adult, so you don't need to be reminded that there are now nearly 80 years of academic data documenting that while there are skilled money managers, they are needles in a haystack of merely lucky ones. Even the truly skilled managers eventually get overwhelmed by the transactional costs incurred by asset bloat. For the decade ending November 2013, for example, Warren Buffett's Berkshire A shares returned 7.63% annually, versus 7.69% for the S&P 500 and, more relevantly, 9.31% for the Dimensional U.S. Large Cap Value Fund (DFLVX), which passively invests in companies with the highest 30 percent of BTM. Over the 15 year period ending November 2013, Berkshire beat the S&P by 1.61%, but lagged DFLVX by almost exactly the same margin.

Does Forecasting Market Returns Do You Any Good?

We're down, then, to market rationality. Do entire markets occasionally get mispriced, and does varying your stock exposure with valuations improve returns? Perhaps the most famous metric used to forecast overall market returns is Shiller's CAPE (cyclically adjusted P/E, or, technically, the ratio of today's market level to the 10-year average of real earnings, expressed in today's dollars). Figure 2-12 plots the forward 10-year returns based on the trailing CAPE.

Clearly, there's a relationship between the CAPE and forward long-term returns. Can you make money off of this? Probably not. The reason why is that valuation metrics are not "stationary." Think of the molecules in a glass of water. If we do not shake the glass, they are stationary. They cannot exist outside of the glass.

Not so with valuation metrics. To understand this better, consider the 10-year real market return as a function of dividend yield between 1871 and 2004, which means that the last relevant dividend for which 10-year forward returns could be observed was in 1994.

Figure 2-12
10-Year Ann'd Real Returns vs Starting CAPE

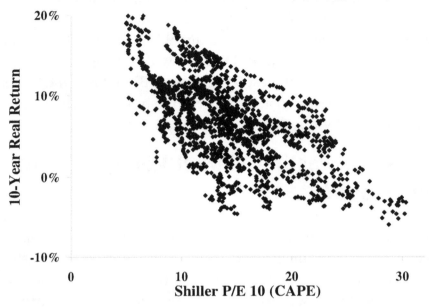

Figure 2-13
10-Year Ann'd Real Returns vs Yield, 1871-1994

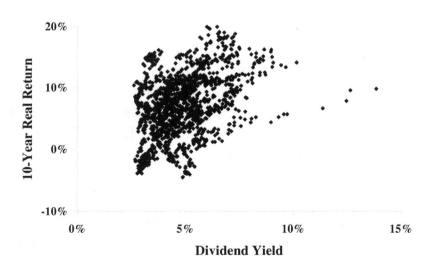

The plot in Figure 2-13 is about as tight as in the previous CAPE plot. Note the sharp cutoff at the lower left, suggesting that if a dividend yield below 3% occurred, returns would be very low.

Now, let's look at the full data set, which extends to 2013, i.e., for which the last relevant dividend yield was in 2003.

Figure 2-14
10-Year Ann'd Real Returns vs Yield, 1871-2003

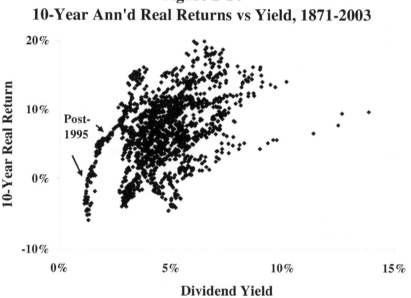

In Figure 2-14 there's a new tail off to the left consisting of starting dividend yields of much less than 3%, for which returns have not been uniformly disastrous. The metaphorical water molecules have just jumped out of the glass, i.e., we're dealing with a nonstationary system.

A comprehensive study of the problem of "nonstationary-ness" was recently made by Welch and Goyal, who looked at multiple valuation and macroeconomic variables and concluded that none were stationary enough to be of any practical use, saying, "These [valuation and economic metrics] would not have helped any investor with access only to available information to profitably time the market."[13]

I'll now introduce three giants in the field: Elroy Dimson, Paul Marsh, and Mike Staunton (hereafter, DMS), who, working at the London Business School, assembled an international database of stock, bond, and bill returns going back, in most cases, to 1900 which they initially published in their seminal work, *Triumph of the Optimists* in 2002. In association with Credit Suisse, since 2009 they have produced annual yearbooks, which have the advantage of being free. I cannot recommend these highly enough.[14]

In the 2013 yearbook, DMS echoed Welch and Goyal by pointing out that market observers frequently fall victim to "the gambler's fallacy," which in terms of forecasting boils down to this: if you look back on x years of market data, at market peaks, valuations are maximal; and at bottoms, they are minimal. Almost by definition, returns following these are minimal and maximal, respectively. In other words, after the fact, valuation metrics *always* look highly predictive. This is a trivial result.

DMS examined the performance of their favored metric, PD_{10}, which is similar to Shiller's CAPE except that it uses dividends, which they consider a more reliable parameter than earnings. They first found modest evidence of returns predictability with their "in-sample" database—that is, over the entire 113-year period they looked at in 21 nations. They then went on to test their results "out-of-sample" by imagining that at any specific point in time during the 113-year period, the investor looked backward, formulated a statistical relationship between valuation and future returns on the data *to that point*, and then tested that with the future series of returns. Result?

Predictability dropped to near zero. (This is similar to what was seen with our examination of the dividend yield of U.S. stocks. Before 1994, you would have predicted disastrous returns when dividends fell much below 3%, which turned out not to be true.) DMS then formulated trading rules that sold equities when forecast real returns based on their model were negative and found that in all 21 nations, return was less than that of simply buying and holding. In other words, a negative regression-based returns forecast contained a lot of "false positives"— periods like the post-1994 example cited above, during which the negative real return prediction was not borne out.

As discouraging as these results were to the strategic asset allocator, the 2011 DMS yearbook examined a different strategy, which separated the 19 markets in their database each year into quintiles (the middle one getting only 3 nations) by dividend yield. They found a monotonically positive relationship as one moved from the low dividend yield quintile, which returned 5.5%, to the high dividend yield quintile, which returned 13.4%.

Further, strategies that lower overall equity allocations at high valuations almost certainly lower risk, not just in terms of plain-vanilla volatility, but also in terms of the sorts of truly awful long-term market declines that are associated with extremely high valuation. Think Japan after 1989's near-triple-digit Nikkei P/E.

Finally, the retired and soon-to-be retired investor will find that the achievement of an LMP-size portfolio will most likely occur following a period of high returns and high valuations. As we'll discuss in much greater detail in chapter 4, when that happy event rolls around, why not take some risk off the table?

Putting together the DMS data with the above life-cycle considerations, then, strategic adjustments to the overall stock and bond mix would seem to make the most sense for older investors with little human capital or savings potential left, not so much for returns enhancement as for risk reduction. On the other hand, for the younger periodic saver who should be socking away as much as possible before, say, age 45 or 50, and for whom poor returns are a blessing, not a curse, adjusting overall equity exposure according to valuations makes little sense.

All investors, in my opinion, will likely benefit from tilting their equity portfolios towards the cheapest nations and regions. While doing this nation-by-nation, as DMS did, is unwieldy, the separation of world equity markets into U.S., developed foreign, and emerging markets segments is useful. Varying allocations among these according to valuation should, over the long term at least, produce salutary results. As of this writing, for example, both developed and emerging foreign equities are selling at lower valuations by most parameters than their U.S. cousins. Accordingly, I believe that the investor should tilt his or her portfolio abroad.

Location, Location, Location

The conventional wisdom is that if your portfolio contains a mix of taxable and tax-sheltered assets, then the bonds belong in the sheltered side, so as to avoid their income being taxed at the ordinary income rate. The same wisdom also says that stocks belong on the taxable side, where they benefit from the lower capital gains and qualified dividend rate. Foreign stocks, moreover, will benefit from the foreign dividend exclusion, which does not apply to sheltered accounts.

While this is a useful rule of thumb, it can be taken too far. To the extent that you wish to rebalance the asset classes in your portfolio, all sales should be done within a sheltered account. If possible, you should house enough of each stock asset class in a sheltered account so that sales may be accomplished free from capital gains taxes. Next, all of the REIT allocation certainly belongs in the sheltered portfolio, since the lion's share of their long-term returns come from nonqualified dividends.

Some maintain that in calculating allocations you should adjust downward the assets in your taxable and traditional IRA/ defined contribution accounts by their estimated future tax exposures. (Roth assets need no discounting.) I largely disagree. To the extent that the assets are fungible among your accounts, it doesn't matter where your assets are. Since there's nothing that prevents you from selling a given dollar amount of equity in your sheltered account and buying it in your taxable account, why should the exact stock/bond allocation of each pool matter?[15]

The *real* difference made by location occurs at the level of overall account returns. In terms of tax liability, Traditional IRA/Defined Contribution > Taxable > Roth IRA. This means that, optimally, you'd like to arrange the expected returns of each account accordingly, with the highest returns (i.e., highest equity allocation) optimally occurring in the Roth, and the lowest returns (i.e., lowest stock allocation) in your Traditional IRA/Defined Contribution pool. To the extent that this is true, it conforms with the stocks-in-the-taxable-side argument. That said, for optimal tax-free rebalancing, unless your Roth IRA is much bigger than your traditional IRA, you're still going to want some stock assets in the latter.

Now that we're more familiar with the basics of allocation, it's time to move on to the largest hurdle between you and a successful investment strategy: the face in the mirror.

CHAPTER 3

THE EVIL NEXUS: MARKET HISTORY, YOUR PORTFOLIO, AND YOUR BRAIN

We are not the rational, calculating beings that economists encapsulate in their models. In particular, human beings respond much better to narratives than to data.

I'll confess that I'm no different. In my previous finance books, I reprised a large body of neuropsychological data that bore on investors' overconfidence and dysfunctional behavior. To give you a little break from all the data, this time around I'm going to tell you some stories that, I think, will prove at least as valuable as the cold, hard facts.

Perhaps the most salient narrative I've come across in a long while was written by reporter Jonathan Cheng for the March 29, 2013 edition of the *Wall Street Journal* about an agreeable, attractive married physician couple, Lucie White and Mark Villa. Wrote Mr. Cheng,

> Feeling "sucker punched," [Ms. White] says, they
> swore off stocks and put their remaining money

in a bank. This week, as the Dow Jones Industrial Average and Standard & Poor's 500-stock index pushed to record highs, Ms. White and her husband hired a financial adviser and took the plunge back into the market. "What really tipped our hand was to see our cash not doing anything while the S&P was going up," says Ms. White, a 39-year-old dermatologist in Houston. "We just didn't want to be left on the sidelines."[1]

While it's all too easy to tut-tut the Villa-White's sell-low, buy-high strategy, we're all subject to the same psychological reactions to financial markets. We're fearful during market plunges and euphoric (or at least comfortable) during frothy times.

Well, almost all of us are. Patients with brain lesions that disconnect their fear-sensing neural structures are emotionally impervious to common external sources of revulsion, including financial loss. They thus react in a more logical manner to price falls. In a classic study, researcher Baba Shiv and colleagues at Stanford, Carnegie Mellon, and University of Iowa took 15 subjects with lesions in these areas and tested them with a task that rewarded risk-taking behavior. They received $2.50 or nothing for a heads or tails coin flip on a given round or a certain $1.00 if they chose not to have the coin toss. Since the coin flip had an expected return of $1.25, the authors concluded that always opting for it was the "rational," preferable choice.

Brain-damaged patients bet on 84% of the rounds, versus only 61% for the controls. Even more striking was the percentage of bets made after a losing round: 85% for the patients—the same as overall and even after winning—versus the 37% of bets made by the control group after its members had lost the previous round.[2]

Since each round consisted of 20 coin flips, simple statistics tells us that there was a 13% chance of flipping less than 8 heads and thus coming out behind. So in truth, whether or not the decision to participate was rational depended on the risk tolerance of the individual subject. But even in that case, each subject would rationally choose, depending on his or her risk tolerance, to participate in *all* or *none* of the rounds. It would be highly irrational to decide to participate (or not) in a given round based on the outcome of the previous round, which the "normal" subjects did to a marked degree, but the brain-damaged subjects did not.

I've observed similar phenomena in both my friends and in professional finance acquaintances. First, the most emotionally intelligent and empathetic people I know tend to be the worst investors. After all, the very definition of "empathy" is the ability to feel the emotions of others, which is deadly in investing. Second, I've observed that those with characteristics of Asperger's syndrome (poor eye contact, an inability to read nonverbal cues, and a very wide dispersion of cognitive skill levels) behave in much the same way as the brain-damaged patients in this study. Probably the most famous example of the Asperger's–investment connection is the remarkable story of a neurology ex-trainee named Michael Burry, whose combination of obsessive-compulsive interest in financial statements and emotional detachment made him one of the few investors who foresaw—and profited from—the GFC.[3]

I pay attention to very few pundits, but we've already come across one of them, Robert Shiller of Yale University. Not only does professor Shiller have a towering command of financial data and financial history, but he also possesses a remarkable track record of forecasting, having predicted the stock market crashes of the early 2000s and the more recent GFC, as well as the longer-lasting housing bubble collapse. (His CAPE spreadsheet, probably the most downloaded Excel file on the planet, makes more than one appearance in this book. And while we're on the subject, former Federal Reserve chairman Alan Greenspan made famous Shiller's use of the term "irrational exuberance" to characterize the 1990s stock bubble.) Here's how the good professor Shiller describes his own psychological makeup:

> People who insulate themselves from the collective consciousness are not very numerous, probably because it's hard to do. I don't follow the crowd as naturally as other people do. I'm kind of "off" there. When I watch a sporting event, I'm always amazed at how intensely people care who wins. As a child, I read [Aldous Huxley's novel] *Brave New World*, and I never wanted to get socialized like that into a caste or clique whose beliefs are reinforced by other people's thinking.[4]

Such imperviousness to the emotions of others is immensely valuable in finance. We've already seen how risk and reward are connected across asset classes. In general and over the long haul, the higher an asset class's return, the higher its risk. The same is also true when comparing one economic era to another. When there's nothing but blue sky, risk seems the lowest. Thus, the expectation is that forward returns should be the lowest. On the other hand, when the economy is going to hell in a handbasket, things seem very risky. Thus, forward returns should be the highest.

History confirms this. The heady years of 1928, 1966, 1999, and 2006 were great times in which to *sell* stocks, while the gloomy periods surrounding 1932, 1982, 2002, and 2009 were fine times in which to *buy* them. In finance, the worst fishing is done on glassy waters, the best on stormy seas.

You Overestimate Your Risk Tolerance

During the Great Depression, a young attorney in Youngstown, Ohio named Benjamin Roth began keeping a diary, and his observations, which chronicle the era's financial milieu, should be required reading for any investor. In 1931, he began noting how inexpensive financial assets of all types—stocks, bonds, mortgages, and real estate—were. On September 2 of that year, he wrote,

> The wise investor will disregard the day-by-day
> fluctuations of the stock market. . . . He must have
> liquid capital in time of depression to buy the
> bargains. . . . It is difficult if not impossible to do
> this but the conservative longtime investor who
> follows the general rule of buying stocks when
> they are selling far below their intrinsic value
> and nobody wants them, and of selling his stocks
> when people are bidding frantically for them at
> prices far above their intrinsic value—such an
> investor will pretty nearly hit the bull's-eye.[5]

Buy low and sell high: simple, right? Problem was, on the day Roth penned that passage, the Dow Jones Industrial Average closed at 137.31, off 64% from its high of 381.17 exactly two years before. (In inflation-adjusted returns, this was approximately equivalent to the 53% nominal fall of the Dow between October 9, 2007 and March 5, 2009.)

Worse—much worse—was to come. On December 11, 1931, when the Dow stood at 79.63, Roth wrote:

> A very conservative young married man with a large family to support tells me that during the past 10 years he succeeded in paying off the mortgage on his house. A few weeks ago, he placed a new mortgage on it for $5,000 and invested the proceeds in good stocks for long-term investment. I think in two or three years he will show a handsome profit. It is generally believed that good stocks and bonds can now be bought at very attractive prices. *The difficulty is that no one has the cash to buy.*[6]

He was more or less right. The Dow eventually bottomed out at 41.22 on July 8, 1932, but three years after Roth wrote that passage, it stood at 100.81, having thrown off dividends of between 4% and 14% along the way. On December 11, 1936, five years after he made his fateful diary entry, the Dow closed at 181.10.

Roth neatly summarized the three requirements for successful investing: "*Patience* to wait for the right moment—*courage* to buy or sell when that time arrives—and *liquid capital.*"[7] At about the same time, Benjamin Graham put it somewhat more perversely, writing, "Those with enterprise haven't the money, and those with money haven't the enterprise, to buy stocks when they are cheap."[8] What he meant is that the plungers— the ones with "enterprise"—had already plunged and lost, and so were cashless, while the ones with money still had it precisely because they never took risks. If this sounds familiar to you, then you get a gold star. These two observers from the 1930s had perceived Vishny and Schleifer's "limits of arbitrage" decades before those later authors clothed Roth and Graham's aphorisms in academic garb.[9]

Let's perform the following exercise. Imagine that it's June 30, 1929, and you plan to retire in 5 years. You now have a $100,000 portfolio that is 75/25 stocks/bonds; $75,000 of stocks, represented by the CRSP 1-10 index, and $25,000 in 5-year Treasury notes, the latter of which you consider to be your "safe money." This $25,000 in bonds, you figure, is enough to pay for 10 years of living expenses, which you estimate at $2,500 per year, a more than adequate cushion in 1929. You're not too concerned that the bonds will last you only 10 years. You figure you'll be able raise additional living expenses by selling stocks, and you resolve to rebalance your portfolio back to its 75/25 composition every year on June 30.

Here's what happens. By June 30, 1930, stocks have fallen by 26%, and you have to sell $6,528 of your precious Treasuries to buy more stocks to bring the portfolio back to 75/25. Over the next year, stocks fall another 26%. On June 30, 1931, you're forced to sell $4,616 more of those even more precious Treasuries.

The next 12 months are yet more disastrous. Stocks fall a further 64%. By June 30, 1932, your Treasury stash is worth $16,959. You calculate that to get back to 75/25, you'll have to sell $8,357 of them—nearly half of the notes—and buy even more stocks. This will leave you just $9,324 in liquid Treasuries—less than four years of living expenses.

What percentage of hypothetical 1932 investors, faced with the apparent imminent demise of capitalism, do you think had the moxie to make that last stock purchase? Far fewer, you can be sure, than made such purchases in early 2009, when the losses were much less.

Had you, the investor, executed that last, rebalancing buy of stocks in 1932, your portfolio would have wound up nudging above the original $100,000 a mere 3 years later. But, of course, you would have had no way of knowing that at the time.

Had you owned a more prudent 50/50 portfolio, the three rebalancing purchases would have reduced the $50,000 of Treasury notes to $29,785 after the June 1932 purchase—a much more comfortable amount that would have given you nearly 12 years of living expenses. Your overall portfolio would have gotten into the black just one year later, in mid-1933.

This exercise is, of course, purely theoretical. Ordinary investors would have had no way of inexpensively obtaining this sort of diversification in the 1930s. Still, it does frame well the issue of repeatedly "averaging down" in a severe and prolonged bear market.

And if there is a moral to this exercise, it is that the older saver, with few working years/human capital remaining, will have extreme emotional difficulty maintaining his or her investment strategy in the face of real adversity. It's better to be safe than sorry with a relatively conservative allocation. Theoretically, the younger investor, as we've already seen, should be in much better shape, if for no other reason than that he'll be deploying his investment capital at low prices—assuming he keeps his job through the hard times.

You Underestimate Uncertainty

An old joke says that it's difficult to make predictions— especially about the future.[10] Since you're an investing adult, you have a good enough working knowledge of history to know just how unpredictable the future is. Who in the year 1800, when neither people nor information traveled faster than the gallop of a horse, would have predicted that within 50 years humans would be speeding over iron rails at 60 miles per hour, or that messages could be sent over thousands of miles of copper wire at the speed of light?[11] Who in 1912 would have predicted that the world would soon be plunged into three decades of cataclysmic warfare that would wipe out the cream of European manhood and destroy the productive capacity of most of the world's developed nations, to say nothing of a global depression that would throw one in four persons out of work? Who in 1978 would guess that China would abruptly embrace market economics and within 40 years challenge the West for economic leadership and wind up owning the lion's share of the U.S. Treasury market, or that the Soviet Union would abruptly collapse? Who in the year 2000 would have predicted the havoc and economic costs triggered by a nearly unforeseeable terrorist event that killed thousands on American soil?

More to the point, while a few investors may have foreseen these developments (as well as the more recent Global Financial Crisis) in some form, any predictions about them appear to fall squarely into the category of proverbial sonnet-producing monkeys. In almost all cases, the subsequent forecasting accuracy of these seers fell rapidly below room temperature. This should not surprise. The complexity of both macroeconomic and political systems is beyond human comprehension, and, plainly put, anyone who forecasts financial or political events more than several years into the future is, almost by definition, a charlatan.

Three decades ago, the world's leading analyst of forecasting accuracy, psychologist Philip Tetlock, examined the performance of 284 recognized experts in economics, domestic and international politics, and military affairs. These mavens made some 28,000 predictions, whose accuracy Tetlock then tested. He found, first and foremost, that experts forecast very poorly, underperforming, in almost all cases, simple statistical rules based on the average frequency and magnitude of past events. These mechanistic base-rate forecasts could be further improved by applying corrections based on simple regression statistics.

Tetlock found that certain characteristics predicted the accuracy of forecasters. He separated them into two broad categories: hedgehogs and foxes, as described by Isaiah Berlin in an essay entitled "The Hedgehog and the Fox." Berlin named his essay after a fragment from the ancient Greek poet Archilochus, who wrote, "The Fox knows many things, but the hedgehog knows one big thing."[12] There are many ways to interpret this statement. Most people take this metaphor to mean that the hedgehog is an expert in one field, an inch wide and a mile deep, while the fox is a dilettante, with a field of expertise that is an inch deep and a mile wide.

Berlin interpreted the metaphor somewhat differently, and Tetlock adopted his narrower definition. Berlin's hedgehog is an ideologue who shoehorns all that he sees into a single grand theory, whereas Berlin's fox considers many competing explanations and often never comes to a firm conclusion among them. Hedgehogs tend to be far more certain of their predictions, which are often extreme. Foxes, in contrast, are fond of weaving together conflicting models and often have a detached, ironic view of events. They are especially "wary of the sound of one analogical hand clapping," i.e., of employing simple analogies.[13]

Tetlock found that foxes usually beat hedgehogs in the forecasting game. In addition, he noted several disturbing trends, all bad news for the hedgehogs. First, understandably, the further out into the future predictions were made, the less accurate they were. Second, the more extreme the predictions were, the less accurate they were. Third, and counterintuitively, beyond a certain general level of knowledge (which Tetlock half jokingly suggested was that possessed by the average *New York Times* reader on a given subject), the greater the expertise, the *less* accurate the forecaster was. All three of these effects were essentially driven by the forecasts of the hedgehogs and were absent among the foxes. Another psychologist, Jonathan Haidt, has identified why better informed and more intelligent observers often make greater forecasting errors. He posits that instead of using their ability and knowledge to update prior beliefs with new data, intelligent observers instead utilize their gifts to rationalize exactly why, even in the face of overwhelming evidence to the contrary, they're still correct.[14]

Tetlock identified yet one more forecasting kiss of death: fame, particularly as manifested in the frequency of appearances on television and quotation in newspapers. Attention by the media contributes to overconfidence (an association that personally worries this author). The media, for its part, is drawn to "boomsters and doomsters," extreme-forecasting hedgehogs, who make for much better sound bites and copy than do level-headed, mushy-mouth foxes. This sets up a positive feedback loop in which the media not only seeks out the most inaccurate forecasters but also worsens their forecasts. In Tetlock's words, "the three principals—authoritative-sounding experts, the ratings-conscious media, and the attentive public—may thus be locked in a symbiotic triangle."[15]

The implication of Tetlock's work for the investor is all too obvious. First and foremost, don't even think about trying to extrapolate macroeconomic, demographic, and political events into an investment strategy. Say to yourself every day, "I cannot predict the future, therefore I diversify." Second, keep his findings in mind every time you come across a plausible sounding talking head or quote in the *Wall Street Journal*. The very fact of media attention implies poor forecasting skills. Then, consider the source. If you regard with suspicion any pundit who regularly is heard on CNBC or NPR or appears in the pages of *USA Today*, you won't go too far wrong.

I'd add another warning sign, and that's the articulateness of the forecaster. Eloquence and erudition carry particularly persuasive power, and in my experience, they usually correlate negatively with forecasting accuracy. For example, both Robert Shiller and Eugene Fama, whose forecasting and analytical ability I've repeatedly mentioned in this book, will never take the trophy in a toastmaster's competition. Be especially suspicious of anyone with a plummy English accent.

Mind Your Memory Banks

Another neurocognitive phenomenon we'll consider has loosely been termed the "memory bank" phenomenon by the late historian and finance writer Peter Bernstein (no relation to this author).[16] Since you're an investing adult, you know all about recency bias—our tendency to be swayed by the most recent data. In the late 1990s, for example, investors believed that high equity returns were the norm, whereas just 20 short years earlier, they believed the opposite. In the late 1970s, people had internalized high inflation as a permanent part of the economic landscape, while over the past several years, the opposite view has prevailed.

When researchers Ulricke Malmendier and Stefan Nagel recently looked at perceptions of inflation among investors over the past several decades, they found a very interesting pattern. The fallacious tendency to extrapolate from the recent past was much more pronounced among the young than among the old. At least in previous decades where forecasts could be verified, older investors had greater forecasting ability.[17] This makes sense. In 1980, the young had lived only in a world of high inflation, which they saw as "normal." In contrast, their elders, many of whom had lived through the deflation of the Great Depression, had a more representative data sample, and so forecast future inflation more accurately.

What are the memories of today's young investor? Besides "permanently" low inflation, they have experienced only low bond yields/high bond prices, and high long-term realized equity returns (except in Japan, which has had nearly a quarter century of lousy ones). None of these will be permanent.

For the young investor, the lesson is clear. Question the "normalcy" of the current environment. You know the present; it's the only one in which you have experienced financial history. But beware! As Malmendier and Nagel imply, the current low inflation may not last forever. If nothing else, at least read about the great hyperinflations of the past. Many books have been written about the events in Weimar Germany between mid-1921 and early 1924, when, for example, the cost of a loaf of bread was measured in millions of marks, then billions of marks, then trillions of marks. Read a few of these and convince yourself that it can happen here.[18] Ask your parents and grandparents what it was like to live through the highly inflationary 1970s. And while you're at it, read about the Great Depression as well. (I'll have some recommendations at the end of the chapter.)

The older investor, with her deeper personal experience and broader knowledge of history, still has lessons to learn, too. She should attempt to "average together" her life experience, casting her mind back to her younger years and convincing herself that her financial memories from those long-ago times are every bit as valid as those from the current environment. In addition, it doesn't hurt senior citizens to read some financial history, no matter how experienced they are.

Don't Be a Prom Queen

We all tend to overemphasize the importance of the peaks in our skill sets. The prom queen inflates the importance of physical appearance and social stature and denigrates those who don't possess them, while the jock judges others on the basis of athletic prowess and locker room demeanor. Of greater relevance here is the intellectual athlete, who measures his family, friends, and peers by their brainpower.

Finance professionals, in particular, tend to overemphasize the importance of mathematical ability. And make no mistake about it, math ability is essential to succeed in investing. Even if you're not engaging in complex calculations, an intuitive feel for the laws of probability and statistical noise are necessary for financial success.

Necessary, but not sufficient. As Warren Buffett famously observed, investing is not a game in which the person with an IQ of 160 beats the person with an IQ of 130. Rather, it's a game best played by those with a broad set of skills that are rich not only in quantitative ability but also in deep historical knowledge, all deployed with Asperger's-like emotional detachment.

The Long Term Capital Management (LTCM) episode of the late 1990s illustrates this point well. An average IQ of 160 may well underestimate the intellectual brawn of its principals, among who were two Nobel Prize winners. The firm's complex arbitrage models, however, were based on a relatively short sample and excluded data that if available would have shown that their bets would eventually blow up.

Which is what happened. Even without these data, the LTCM whiz kids forgot Isaac Newton's observation that he could calculate the motion of the heavenly bodies but not the madness of men. From time to time, the animal spirits take over the markets and wreck most schemes based on leverage and liquidity, both of which disappear during a crisis. (The LTCM principals may also have suffered from "Tetlock syndrome," which is characterized by highly focused hedgehog-like skills and is exacerbated by fame and overconfidence.)

I suspect that this book's readers include many engineers, scientists, and I.T. people—all types who are good with numbers. If you fit this description, then the foregoing discussion is a plea to fill in what may be the shallow areas of your skills: a working knowledge of financial history and healthy dollop of self-awareness about your discipline under fire. The accompanying text box will give you a good start.

A Good Start in Financial History

You really can't learn enough financial history. The following, listed in descending order of importance, are landmarks in the field.

Edward Chancellor. *Devil Take the Hindmost.* New York: Farrar, Straus, and Giroux, 1999. What manias look like; how to recognize—and hopefully avoid—irrational exuberance.

Benjamin Roth. *The Great Depression: A Diary.* New York: PublicAffairs, 2009. What the bottoms look like; how to keep your courage and your cash up.

Roger G. Ibbotson and Gary P. Brinson. *Global Investing.* New York: McGraw-Hill, 1993. Five hundred years of hard and fiat money, inflation, and security returns in a small, easy-to-read package.

Adam Fergusson. *When Money Dies.* New York: PublicAffairs, 2010; Frederick Taylor. *The Downfall of Money.* New York: Bloomsbury Press, 2013. What real inflation looks like. Be afraid, very afraid.

Benjamin Graham. *Security Analysis.* New York: McGraw-Hill, 1996. You're not a pro until you've read Graham "in the original"—the first edition, published in 1934. An authentic copy in decent condition will run you at least a grand. Fortunately, McGraw-Hill brought out a facsimile reprint in 1996.

Charles Mackay. *Extraordinary Popular Delusions and the Madness of Crowds.* Petersfield, U.K.: Harriman House Ltd., 2003. If you were smitten with *Devil Take the Hindmost,* you'll love this nineteenth-century look at earlier manias.

Sydney Homer and Richard Sylla. *A History of Interest Rates,* 4th ed. Hoboken, NJ: John Wiley & Sons, 2005. Loan markets from 35th-century B.C. Sumer to the present.

CHAPTER 4

WHEN TO HOLD 'EM, WHEN TO FOLD 'EM: A LIFETIME ASSET-ALLOCATION TRAJECTORY

We now have all the tools we need to answer the three basic questions of life-cycle planning: How much should you save? How should your assets be deployed? How should you spend them down?

I'm going to assume that your main investing goal is retirement, for which the phases of saving and consumption can span seven or eight decades. I will not cover saving for college expenses, the savings and consumption phases of which will last at most a few decades. Educational saving is a highly telescoped version of retirement and thus is a radically different calculation that involves a higher exposure to safe and liquid assets. I'll also ignore the management of endowments and other perpetuities, which, on the other hand, has no savings phase but rather an infinite consumption phase, the dynamics of which are, once again, very different from those of retirement savings.

We could conduct, as I did in my prior books, complex spreadsheet and Monte Carlo exercises to predict just how many years it will take to reach a realistic retirement nest egg or at what rate it can be spent down. These calculations bring to mind the following joke: Q. How do we know that economists have a sense of humor? A. They use decimal points. There are just too many variables to pretend great precision: career and salary trajectory, personal and family health (and health expenses), to say nothing of the vicissitudes of the markets and of that cruelest mistress of all, human history. You might as well try to mathematically model your love life.

So, in this book, I am eschewing decimal points for the back of the envelope labeled "liability matching portfolio" (LMP). If there is one concept that is central to this book, it is that of the LMP: the amount of money necessary to cover a retiree's future basic living expenses.

Let's start with someone who needs $55,000 per year to cover these who has a $5,000 annual pension and expects $25,000 in annual Social Security payments. Will the future young retiree actually get his $25,000 in Social Security? Maybe not. Without significant reform, he will receive only about 75% to 80% of the currently promised benefit. He thus should expect to get just $20,000 in annual Social Security payments and figure on needing an additional $30,000 per year ($55,000 of needs minus $5,000 pension and $20,000 Social Security) for his and his spouse's living expenses. This $30,000 per year constitutes his "residual living expenses" (RLE)—the amount he'll need to live on after receiving his Social Security payments and pension benefits.

The most venerable rule of thumb is William Bengen's "4 percent rule," which suggests that 4% of a nest egg, adjusted upwards for inflation, can safely be spent in retirement.[1] The problem with this rule is that the securities landscape in 2014 looks very different than it did when Bengen based his analysis on the historically high stock returns of the 1926–1994 period. Burning through 4% may have been realistic in 1994, when stocks were selling at lower multiples and bonds still had high real yields. But in an era with lower expected equity returns and negative real short-term fixed income yields, this rule may now be far too optimistic. A 60-year-old retiree, for example, should probably be spending no more than 3% of a balanced portfolio nest egg each year.

If you learn nothing else from this book, remember this: the purpose of your investment plan is to accumulate an LMP tailored to your retirement needs. Your LMP, once achieved, should be sacred and should never, ever take a back seat to your desire for higher returns. The purpose of investing is not to simply optimize returns and make yourself rich. The purpose is to not die poor. Warren Buffett most succinctly expressed this concept in a commentary on the 1998 bankruptcy of Long Term Capital Management: "To make the money they didn't have and they didn't need, they risked what they did have and did need."[2] In other words, once you've won the game, the wisest thing is to stop playing. This doesn't mean to sell all your stocks the moment you reach your LMP. Rather, it means not to retire until you've reached it, and if you do acquire it before you retire, to start moving the risk out of your portfolio.

An annuity or a TIPS ladder comes pretty close to the definition of an LMP, which is defined as a secure income stream that will meet your retirement needs. But neither of these is perfect. Annuities have their problems. In the first place, they provide no cushion for emergencies. More importantly, there is significant risk that your insurance company (or even multiple companies, if you've spread default risk around) will fail, particularly during a financial crisis.

Many cite state guarantees of annuity payments, but in a systemic crisis, those will not even be a speed bump on the road to default. I'm unimpressed by the argument "It's never happened before." Prior to September 11, 2001, one could have said the same thing about a mass terrorism incident on American soil, and just as the 1993 attempted bombing of the World Trade Center should have been a wake up call, so, too, should the GFC be a warning about the vulnerability of insurance companies in a complex, linked financial system.

A TIPS ladder, on the other hand, has a much lower risk of default and can supply emergency funds if needed, but it carries another risk: that you and your spouse may live more than 30 years in retirement. Finally, both annuities and a TIPS ladder carry the additional risk of government manipulation of the CPI.

For now, we'll assume that for the age 65 retiree, *the 65-year-old's LMP needs 25 years of RLE.* In the case of the hypothetical retiree discussed above, this is $30,000 multiplied by 25, or $750,000.

In 2013, because of negative real interest rates, the LMP came much more dearly, at closer to 30 years of expense. Although real interest rates have risen at the long end, now is still probably not the best time to plunge headlong into an LMP. As we'll get to later, the cheapest LMP you can "buy" is to spend down your retirement fund in order to delay taking Social Security until you reach age 70. That increases your payments by 8% for each year of delay, but it carries the risk that Congress may vote to decrease the benefit, in which case you might be better off starting benefits sooner rather than later.

Figure 4-1
Year Began Work to a Full LMP (= 20 Years
Full Salary) with S&P 500

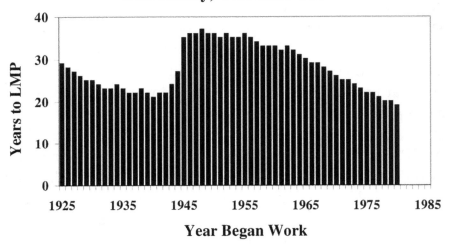

Figure 4-1 shows a theoretical exercise in which we calculate how many years it took, at historical real rates of return, to accumulate an LMP at a savings rate of 20% of salary by investing in the S&P 500.

Let's unpack this a bit. First, for the sake of simplicity, I've assumed that the worker in question receives no Social Security or pension, so her LMP is 25 years of her living expenses. If she can afford to invest 20% of her salary and is able to live on the remaining 80% of it, her LMP is thus 20 years of inflation-adjusted salary. If she began working and saving in 1926 and invested that 20% in the U.S. stock market, it took her 29 years to accumulate this amount. The most favorable year to start investing was 1980, after which accumulating her LMP took just 19 years. The least favorable year was 1948, following which it took 37 years. This paradigm, of course, is a simplification that ignores Social Security income and the fact that living expenses in retirement are often lower than in middle age, but it still serves to illustrate the vagaries of retirement savings.

I've used an all-stock investment plan simply because the average person can't accumulate an LMP consisting of 25 years of RLE by investing in safe fixed-income assets. In order to reach your LMP, you are, like most savers, going to have to take risk.

The good news, as we've already discussed, is that stocks are not as risky for younger investors as they seem at first blush to be. This is *not* because stocks "become less risky with time." This old chestnut is an artifact of the calculation of long-term returns on an annualized basis. Since 1926, for example, the extremes of 30-year annualized returns of the S&P 500, calculated monthly, have been 14.78% and 7.80%. This doesn't sound so bad when placed next to the high and low returns for single 12-month periods, +162.88% and -67.57%. The problem here is that we're comparing apples and oranges—annualized returns versus a single annual return. The dispersion of *total* 30-year returns—a high of +6,153% and a low of +851%—is much higher than for the annual returns. Moreover, over the long run, markets usually recover nicely from annual returns of even -67.57%. But you only get one shot at 30-year returns, and if you get a bad one during the distribution phase, you may die poor.

The young saver, of course, should get down on her knees and pray for bad returns, since these will enable her to buy shares on the cheap. By contrast, the retiree desires high returns, since she cannot make up the losses with further savings.

This is clearly shown in Figure 4-1, where the shortest paths to an LMP started in the late 1930s and the late 1970s, both of which came at the tail end of very poor returns series. Ideally, you should start your savings career during a severe economic downturn that depresses share prices. (This recommendation somewhat heroically assumes that you will find and keep a well-paying job during hard times.) Figure 4-1 also encapsulates an ugly reality that gets almost no attention. Anyone who saves to retire of necessity plays demographic roulette. The markets may be kindest, paradoxically, to those who began their working careers during periods of distress, such as the grim years of the 1930s and 1970s (or at least to those who could find work). Those who began to work in boom times, on the other hand, often do not fare well. A short work career—think of a highly trained surgical subspecialist who does not begin his or her career until age 35—magnifies the chances of a poor demographic draw.

This paradox gets to the major flaw in the human capital/ investment capital paradigm, which is that these two forms of capital are not independent, but are, in fact, strongly linked. Sadly, peaks and troughs in both tend to occur together.

The model shown in Figure 4-1 seems at first to be heroically premised: that you're actually able to save 20% of salary and then earn the historical returns of the S&P 500. And even with that best-case scenario, you may have to save for more than 3 decades to get to your LMP. But remember, this model assumes no Social Security or pension, so for most savers, things aren't that grim.

So with an aggressive savings and investment strategy, you've got a decent shot at a reasonable retirement. With assets that carry no risk, you're far less likely to succeed. If the analysis in Figure 4-1 is rerun with the real return of 5-year Treasury notes, it takes between 40 and 62 years to accumulate the LMP—roughly twice as long as with stocks. Further, the shorter time to the LMP (in the 40-year range) with 5-year Treasury notes occurred during a time of very high real bond returns in the latter half of the period, something not likely to occur going forward.

This makes perfect sense, of course. At present, it's a struggle even to find safe bonds with an expected real return of zero. At a zero real return, the calculation is simple. If you save 20% of your salary for 50 years, you've accumulated just 10 years of salary, or 12.5 years of living expenses. Since you've been living on 80% of your salary, unless you'll be able to draw a large amount of your RLE from Social Security and pensions, 12.5 years of savings gets you nowhere near an LMP.

This discussion suggests an unpleasant reality. We can't all retire at 65, and perhaps not even at 70, no matter how much we save on average. At first blush the reason for this seems obvious. It's generally agreed that Americans aren't saving enough. For example, the latest report out of the Employee Benefit Research Institute shows that before about 1985, the U.S. savings rate averaged 8% to 9% during peacetime. (During the Great Depression, the savings rate fell as low as 1.9%, while the forced savings brought on by shortages and rationing during World War II pushed it as high as 26%.)

After 1985, the savings rate plunged again, this time as low as 1.4% in 2005, before the GFC knocked some sense into consumers and it rose again to 5.9% in 2009.[3]

But as we've seen, 6%, or even the 8% to 9% of the pre-1985 era, is not enough. The EBRI data on 401(k) balances, for example, show that at the end of 2011, employees in their 60s had shockingly low median balances: $53,063 for employees with 5 to 10 years of service and $159,447 for those lucky enough to have accumulated 20 to 30 years of tenure. These figures correspond to perhaps 2 to 5 years worth of RLE, or, more cynically, even for those on the job longer, less than the average out-of-pocket medical expenses for a retired married couple.[4]

But even increasing the savings rate is no panacea. Let's say that every worker woke up tomorrow morning and began stashing away 25% of his or her paycheck. In very short order, the reduced consumer spending would crater corporate profits and stock prices. The trade-off between increased savings and the resultant depression in asset prices (from lower consumer spending) is a mind-boggling macroeconomic calculation, but a fast look at Japan, with its high savings rate, is not encouraging.

We can trace our current problem all the way back to Germany in 1883, when Otto von Bismark, wishing to co-opt the Socialists, declared age 65 to be the retirement age. We have been stuck with this age ever since. In an era without adequate nutrition, antibiotics, high blood pressure medicine, and rudimentary occupational safety, only a small percentage of people survived much beyond that age. Even when Franklin Roosevelt signed the Social Security Act in 1935, relatively few Americans lived to qualify, and there were 40 workers for every beneficiary. The first Social Security check was made out to ex-schoolteacher and legal secretary Ida May Fuller, who retired in 1939 after paying into the system for just 3 years. On January 31, 1940, she received her first check, for $22.54, having paid in just $24.75. By the time she died at age 100, she had collected $22,888.92.

Ida was, especially for that age, a spectacular outlier. Today, the median life expectancy for men is 75 years; it's 80 for women. Currently, there are 3 workers for every retiree. By 2050, there will be only 1.5 workers supporting each retiree.

Thornton Parker raised the demographic issue in *What if the Boomers Can't Retire*, as did Robert Arnott and Anne Casscells in an academic piece in *Financial Analysts Journal*.[5] Imagine, if you will, a desert island on which there are only 5 inhabitants—4 workers and one older retired person. Each of the four workers does several odd jobs: growing food, building shelter, providing rudimentary medical care, and the like.

One day, 1 of the remaining 4 workers turns sixty-five and decides that he, too, wishes to retire. Instead of each worker supporting 0.25 retirees, he now must support 0.67 retirees. Not only that, but the island's total GDP and per-capita GDP would each fall by 25%. What do you suppose the response of the remaining 3 workers would be to an apparently healthy-looking colleague who demanded that they support his idleness?

Let us further assume that the medium of exchange on the island is coconuts and that a retiree, instead of accepting charity from the workers, funds his nonproductive years by accumulating enough coconuts. In doing so, he has done nothing to increase the economic output of the island. Now that he must spend the coconuts, the island will find an increased number of them chasing 25% fewer goods and services. A predictable bear market in coconuts ensues, along with dramatically more expensive goods and services. Worse yet, to the extent that he has planned ahead and saved, the frugal retiree sows discord, for even if he has accumulated enough coconuts to counteract the effects of higher prices, he has raised prices for everyone else in the process.

This example was not pulled out of thin air. The 4:1 and 3:2 ratios of workers to retirees are about what the case was in 1990 and what the case will be in 2050, respectively. It does not matter whether the retirees are paying the workers with coconuts, dollar bills, stock certificates, or Krugerrands. At the end of the day, the method of savings/payment is irrelevant. As the number of retirees increases, the goods and services produced by the remaining workers become thin on the ground. In this case, it does not matter how much retirees have saved—the value of their coconuts, dollar bills, stock certificates, and Krugerrands must fall to the point where the workers are finally willing to take them in exchange for those goods and services.

Arnott and Casscells concluded that we didn't have a *savings* crisis, but rather a *demographic* crisis. We will not be rescued by increased voluntary or enforced savings. The only viable solution is for workers to work longer. We've already started down that road by raising the full retirement age (FRA) for future Social Security benefits to 67 for those born after 1959. Even so, we have a ways to go. In order to keep the current worker-to-retiree ratio at 3:1, Arnott and Casscells estimate that the retirement age will gradually have to be raised to 73. The government need take no action. Politically, it will prove far simpler to let low securities prices and low savings force older Americans to postpone retirement.

The metaphor that comes most easily to mind here is of two men being chased by a bear. Says the first man to the second, "It looks like we can't outrun this bear." Replies the second, "I don't have to outrun the bear. I just have to outrun you." Chances are, the mere fact that you've gotten this far in this book likely means that you'll find yourself in the position of the second man, able to save and retire mainly because those around you are running so slowly.

Stock Exposure throughout the Life Cycle

The previous discussion can be summarized as follows. Unless you can start saving a very large portion—more than 30% of your salary—you're not going to be able to retire by investing in safe assets. You're going to have to take some risk in order to accumulate a reasonable nest egg.

To reiterate, the perceived riskiness of stocks depends on where in the life cycle you are. Rather than review the extensive literature on consumption-based models, I'm going to illustrate the riskiness of stocks by revisiting the Great Depression with the same historical worst-case scenario: the years following January 1929, which included not only the brutal bear market that ended in July of 1932 but also a second bear market in 1937–1938 that saw stock prices fall by nearly half.

Imagine three employees of an organization that prospered reasonably well throughout the Great Depression—say a film studio or insurance company. Let's start with one, a chap named Fred Forty-Five, a middle-career executive who decided at the beginning of 1929 that he'd socked away enough in stocks to fund his retirement a decade or two thence and could now spend all his salary. I'll represent stocks during this period with the CRSP 1-10 all-stock universe.

Fred had quite the ride during that decade, seeing the inflation-adjusted value of his portfolio fall by 74% by the end of June 1932 (79% when measured in nominal terms), recover nicely by January 1937, only to fall by another 48% between then and March 1938. There were further fluctuations above and below inflation-adjusted par after that, and finally, at the end of 1943, when he was 60, the inflation-adjusted value of his portfolio finally and permanently fully regained its 1929 purchasing power. So he did fine, since he did not have to sell down his nest egg for living expenses along the way. Over that harrowing decade and a half, he had lost a lot of sleep, but his real wealth was once again intact. Now that's risk in action!

But Fred's sleepless nights were nothing compared with what happened to Sam Sixty-Five, who retired in January 1929. Sam thought he could easily spend an inflation-adjusted 8% of his portfolio per year. Unfortunately, he ran out of money in early 1938. Had he cut his spending to 7%, 6%, 5%, and even 4%, he would have run out of money in late 1938, 1941, 1943, and 1950, respectively. A 30-year portfolio survival would have required a spending rate of less than 3.6%.

Finally, Ted Twenty-Five, a junior executive, began saving and investing 20% of his $6,000 salary—an inflation-adjusted $100 per month—in common stocks in January 1929. That summer, he was particularly taken by an interview that *Ladies' Home Journal* had done with John Raskob, a senior executive at General Motors. The interview, entitled "Everybody Ought to be Rich" and shown to him by his wife, included this memorable passage:

> Suppose a man marries at the age of twenty-three and begins a regular savings of fifteen dollars a month—and almost anyone who is employed can

do that if he tries. If he invests in good common
stocks and allows the dividends and rights to
accumulate, he will at the end of twenty years
have at least eighty thousand dollars and an
income from investments of around four hundred
dollars a month. He will be rich. And because
anyone can do that I am firm in my belief that
anyone not only can be rich but ought to be rich.[6]

In 1929, poor Mr. Raskob didn't have access to spreadsheets,
or even a financial calculator. The scenario he so blithely
tossed out—240 sequential monthly inflows of $15 per month
compounding at a given rate—would have required days of
computation with logarithm tables, so he probably didn't know
that turning this inflow into $80,000 over 20 years required an
annualized return of 26%.

Ted Twenty-Five, like the rest of the article's readers, didn't
realize that Raskob was blowing smoke. Throughout the Great
Depression, Ted kept plowing an inflation-adjusted $100 into
the market every month, figuring that he'd be buying in at the
bottom sooner or later, as indeed he did. By the time he retired
in December 1958, Ted had accumulated $335,179 in 1929-current
dollars—worth $2,707,000 today—more than enough for him to
retire on.

But this is not a discussion about return. For the moment,
we're talking about risk. The wealth trajectories of these three
hypothetical investors demonstrate just what "risk" means
to investors at different stages of their life cycle. For savers
like Ted, it's not too much to say that stock market volatility
was a blessing, not a curse. Because he invested through two

terrible bear markets, young Ted accumulated so many shares at low prices that he was able to retire in comfort. The crushing volatility of those two awful markets was Ted's best friend.

To further explore the concept of risk under periodic saving, I've performed a thought experiment in which I conjured up an investor who saved an inflation-adjusted $100 per month for 30 years—360 months—during each of the possible overlapping 30-year periods between 1871 and late 2013. Figure 4-2 shows that during this period, it was impossible to have a net real loss of capital (i.e., wind up with less than $36,000 at the end of the period) for the simple reason that real equity returns were so high—6.83%.

Figure 4-2
End Real Value of $36,000 Input

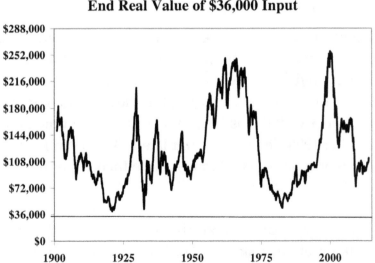

You're an investing adult, so you realize that it's bogus to use historical data beginning in 1871—a highly favorable period for the U.S. stock market, the world's long-run returns champion.

Figure 4-3
Failure to Reach Target vs. Real Equity Return

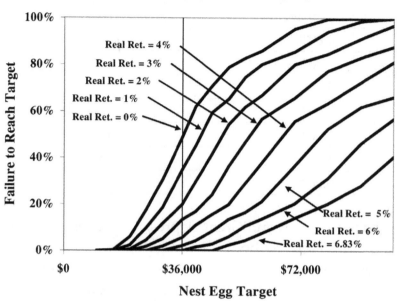

Figure 4-3 remedies this problem by plotting on the y-axis the percentage failure rate (defined by amounts on the x-axis), at given real equity returns ranging from 0% to the realized real historical return of 6.83% for this 360 x $100 saving model. The table on page 132 summarizes from this plot the percentage of the time that the saver failed to realize a final real portfolio value of $36,000 (that is, failed to conserve his spending power). At any reasonable real equity return, the chance of failure is relatively low, but not zero. For example, at a real return of 3%, the chance of failure (winding up with less than a real $36,000) is about 1 in 7, and less than 1 in 50 of winding up with less than a real $25,000. At the same time, there is a 1 in 8 chance of winding up with a portfolio of more than a real $100,000, portfolio odds that most investors would be willing to take.

Real Equity Return	Failure to Conserve Real $36,000 of Consumption
6.83% (historical)	0.00%
6.00%	0.07%
5.00%	2.21%
4.00%	5.75%
3.00%	13.57%
2.00%	19.91%
1.00%	35.03%
0.00%	48.89%

Now, back to our second Great Depression retirement example, middle-aged Fred. Although his nest egg came through fine in the end, he suffered from tanker-car quantities of stomach acid and severe insomnia along the way. Volatility was most definitely not his friend. (And truth be told, as illustrated in Figure 1-3 from chapter 1, for every Fred who gritted his teeth and held on, many more sold near the bottom, doing themselves irreparable damage in the process.)

And for Sam Sixty-Five the retiree, volatility was not merely nerve-wracking. It was financially fatal.

The overarching lesson of these three men, then, is that the older you are, and the fewer working years you have ahead of you (or, to use a four-bit term, the less human capital you have), the riskier stocks are. For the young saver, stocks are not that risky. For those in the middle phase of their financial life, they are quite risky. For the retiree, they are as toxic as Three Mile Island.

Although periodically investing small amounts over a long period, à la Ted Twenty-Five, *does* lower risk, this comes at a cost: it most often produces lower returns than are achieved by investing a lump sum. This is because the time-weighted amount exposed to the market with a lump-sum investment is so much higher than with periodic investing. Ted Twenty-Five, of course, has no choice in the matter; he's going to have to invest periodically.

Two finance academics, Ian Ayres and Larry Nalebuff, have suggested that Ted could have improved his returns by leveraging his portfolio early in his savings career. Their recommended strategy is the purchase of long-duration index call options, which produces the stock exposure plot that is shown in Figure 4-4.

Figure 4-4
Ayres/Nalebuff Life-cycle Paradigm

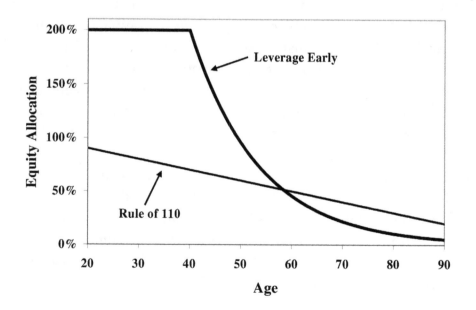

Ayres and Nalebuff proposed a complex allocation trajectory that maintains 2-to-1 stock leverage until an investor is in his or her early 40s, followed by gradual deleveraging to a low stock exposure in retirement. They then compared that strategy to two others: one an allocation path similar to the Rule of 110, the other a strategy of a constant 100% stock exposure.

Using Robert Shiller's securities return series going back to the nineteenth century, Nalebuff and Ayres found that in almost all cases, their leverage-early strategy did better than a strategy of 100% stocks. The all-stock portfolio, in turn, did much better than the traditional Rule of 110 strategy of adjusting down stock exposure with age (that is, at age 25, stock exposure = 110 - 25 = 85%; at age 80, stock exposure = 110 – 80 = 30%). In fact, even the worst returns for the leverage-early strategy were better than those for the Rule of 110.

But, you might ask, didn't leveraging at 2-to-1 "margin out" during the catastrophic three-year bear market from 1929 to 1932 or even in the 2007 to 2009 one, which saw a loss of more than 50%? No. The constant stream of contributions prevented younger investors from being sold out, while older ones had by that point eliminated their leverage. During severe bear markets, as the authors point out, investors who are leveraged but young will lose "a large percentage of a small amount."[7, 8]

But isn't the success of their strategy just an artifact of the high historical returns of U.S. stocks? What if the stock market delivers lower future returns? Nalebuff and Ayres also ran their simulations using the returns of British stocks, which had lower returns, and with Japanese stocks, which suffered a brutal bear market—they're still in it—after 1989. In both cases, leverage-early still beat both the constant 100% equity exposure and the more traditional Rule of 110 strategy.[9]

Ayres and Nalebuff, to say nothing of the examples of Ted, Fred, and Sam, suggest that young savers should maximally expose themselves to stocks. I'm not a big fan, though, of establishing a leveraged position in long-duration options (Ayres and Nalebuff's favored leverage mechanism), which I see as undiversified and prone to counterparty risk in the long run. If you're going to take maximum risk, it makes more sense to do so with exposure to the classic risk factors: market, small, value, momentum, profitability, and whatever else the academics find, as they surely will, in the future.

There's a big problem with the theoretically appealing concept of hyperaggressive stock exposures early in the life cycle. Young investors, in my experience, may well have *lower* tolerance for risk than older investors do. The academic literature on risk tolerance and age is ambiguous on the subject, but the data are crystal clear on one point: Risk tolerance increases with wealth. A 50% fall in the value of a 401(k) plan whose $25,000 balance represents the major liquid asset of a young saver will devastate her. She'll likely be gun-shy about stocks in the future, her multimillion-dollar human capital notwithstanding.[10]

I seriously doubt that most young and inexperienced investors have the moxie to stick with such a strategy through boom and bust. A good compromise, especially for the young investor with a small balance, would be a less aggressive mix that is in the range of 50/50. Sooner rather than later, her courage will be tested by a severe bear market. A young investor's first encounter with a significant market decline serves mainly to ascertain her true risk tolerance. Her responses to the decline define the policy allocation that takes her to age 45 or 50. Does she panic and sell? Then certainly her long-term policy allocation to stocks should be less than 50%. If she holds fast but does not have the stomach to buy more, then 50% is likely about right. And if she piles in, then I say, "God bless." Perhaps she can increase her policy allocation to stocks to 60% to 80%. The next few decades should allow her to test, adjust, and repeat the process at least a few more times.

Asset Allocation throughout the Life Cycle

We've now put together the investor's life-cycle asset-allocation trajectory. First, during the early years, when human capital, and thus the inflow into the portfolio, greatly exceeds the portfolio size, the young investor determines her risk tolerance—her "sleeping point portfolio": the stock allocation at which she is able to not only stick with her equity holdings in the face of a severe bear market but continues to add to them with savings. She then sticks to this allocation, building up her portfolio value as rapidly as she can. The ultimate goal is to achieve the LMP: 25 years of residual living expenses (RLE).

The first question to be answered, then, is what percentage of your retirement living expenses will be covered by Social Security and pensions. If you're lucky enough (or more likely, frugal enough) to live entirely on Social Security and pensions, then, aside from emergency money, you've already got your LMP, and you're really not managing your assets for yourself, but rather for your heirs and charities and for Uncle Sam. (I do, by the way, see the old boy as a worthy recipient. Without him, all of us, even those who see ourselves as "self-made" men and women, would be nowhere.)

And if you're unlucky enough (or have high enough living expenses) that Social Security and pensions won't pay a significant percentage of your retirement costs, then the foregoing discussion suggests that if you save 20% of your salary, it will take as little as 20 years, or as many as 60 years, depending on the gods of finance and history and on your asset allocation, to accumulate an adequate LMP. Don't shoot me! I'm only the messenger.

Most people are about halfway between these two extremes. If half of your living expenses will be paid by Social Security and a pension, then your LMP will need to total about 10 years of your full salary at a savings rate of 20%, as opposed to the 20 years used to plot Figure 4-2.

Figure 4-5
Year Began Work to LMP of 10 Years Full Salary with All S&P 500

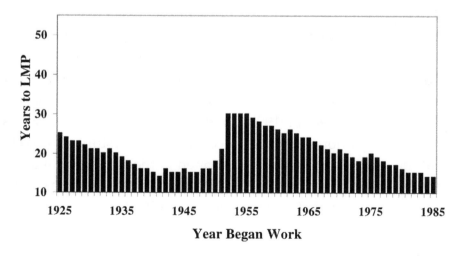

Figures 4-5 through 4-7 show what happens when we run this sort of analysis for the "half-LMP" scenario (half of living expenses met by Social Security payments and pensions).

Figure 4-6
Year Began Work to LMP of 10 Years Full Salary
with 50/50 Portfolio

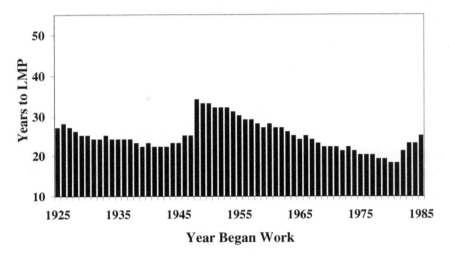

Both Figure 4-1 from earlier in this chapter (years to accumulate 20 years of salary) and Figure 4-5 (years to accumulate 10 years of salary) demonstrate a "waterfall" phenomenon of ever shorter accumulation times until an unlucky cohort "goes over the falls," i.e., just misses making their LMP at a bull market peak, as happened in 1999. In this regard, Figure 4-7 looks especially ominous for fixed-income-only investors. It's likely that the same thing is about to happen to them as a bull market in bonds that has now lasted a third of a century seems to be entering into advanced senescence, if not its death throes.

Figure 4-7
Year Began Work to LMP of 10 Years Full
Salary with 5-Year Treasury Notes

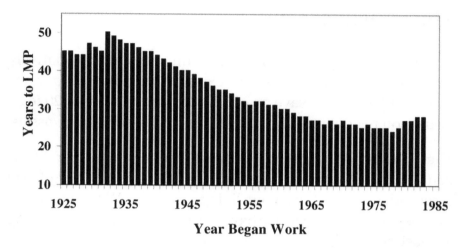

To summarize the results of this section's model of a 20% savings rate with various asset allocations:

Amount of Retirement Income from Pensions and Social Security	Number of Years Required to Reach LMP with 100% S&P 500	Number of Years Required to Reach LMP with 50/50	Number of Years Required to Reach LMP with 100% Bonds
None	19 to 37	27 to 46	40 to 62
Half	14 to 30	18 to 34	24 to 50
All	Home Free!	Home Free!	Home Free!

The message of this table is clear. Unless Social Security and pensions will pay a large percentage of your retirement expenses *or* you are a prodigious saver, you have a very long and hard road ahead of you.

The Toughest Call

The accumulation phase of the investing life-cycle is relatively straightforward: unless either extreme frugality or a huge income allow you to save nearly 50% of your salary for 20 to 30 years, you're going to have to invest in at least some risky assets.

The distribution (retirement) phase of your investing life is equally straightforward. With luck, you'll have an LMP of safe assets adequate to fund your living expenses. With even more luck beyond that, you'll also have a risk portfolio (RP) containing at least some risky assets for your aspirational needs, heirs, charities, and, if you're very patriotic or haven't planned your estate well, for Uncle Sam.

It's the middle phase—the transition between a risky accumulation portfolio and the retirement LMP—that's the trickiest. If you're fortunate, you'll get a low-returns-first, high-returns-last sequence and reach your LMP when you're relatively young, perhaps as early as your late 40s or mid-50s. Or it might not happen until right before you retire. Or, if you get an especially awful draw—a high-returns-first, poor-returns-last sequence—you might never get there.

Midlife, then, is the most difficult and uncertain phase in the investing life cycle. It marks the transition between an aggressive investment stance of the early years, when the long-term risks of stock investing are relatively low, and the conservative investment stance of the later years, when stocks potentially become toxic in the long term. Early in one's investing lifetime, the focus is on rapidly building up assets. In other words, a rich wage stream and future human capital mitigate the risks of owning equity. But, later in life, when an investor's human capital is depleted, there is little margin for error.

At some point, then, *even if you haven't reached your LMP*, you should start lightening up on equities. If, for example, you're 60 years old, want to retire at 65, are saving 20% of your salary, and currently have a nest egg sufficient to pay for only 9 years of RLE, then, under normal circumstances, a bond portfolio's investment return in the remaining 5 years should provide you with 10 to 12 years of RLE by age 65. If you're too aggressively invested and suffer a bad initial draw of equity returns, you may suffer losses that will make you run out of money much sooner than even 10 years.

As we already saw above, unless you are an Olympic-class saver, you can't get there from here with riskless assets. If you cannot save at least 20% of your *pretax* salary beginning at age 25 or obtain a high risk-free return on what you invest (or both), you will not be able to retire until shortly before you are pushing up the daisies. Oh, those lucky Boomers, who vacuumed up double-digit CDs and Treasuries in the 1970s and 1980s.

Consider the following: At present (2014), risk-free assets have an expected real return that is lower than zero. Over longer periods, a real 2% is the best you can do. Further, your "hedonic set point" will change with time. Worker productivity, wages, and per-capita GDP all grow at a real rate of about 2% per year, as will your expectations. Would you be happy with a 1960 standard of living? When everyone else has an iPad and smart phone, can you live without these? Thus, if the real return of a retirement portfolio invested in safe assets is, optimistically, 2%, then one year of earnings will buy exactly one year of hedonically adjusted retirement. If you plan 30 years of retirement, and you want to do it with CDs, plain Treasuries, and TIPS, you'll have to save half of your salary during the three decades that you *are* working.

Unless you're comfortable with such depressing retirement math, you're going to have to take some risk—à la age equals bonds, Nalebuff and Ayres, or tilting towards small, value, momentum, profitability, or whatever other returns/risk factors you have available. A fast spreadsheet run shows, for example, that if you want to retire at age 70 without Social Security or a pension, you'll have to start working at age 25, save 20% of your salary, and earn a 3.5% real return on your portfolio over the intervening years. If you want to retire at age 60, you'll either have to earn a 6% return or save 30% of your salary. What if you don't start working until age 35? In that case, you'll have to get a 3.5% real rate of return, save 30% of your salary, *and* be willing to retire at age 70. To start work at 35 and retire at age 60, you'll have to save over *half* of your salary. And don't count on a 6% real return, or even a 3.5% real return, by investing in safe assets. You're not going to get it.

When, and how, do you transition from a risky young-investor strategy to the low-risk retiree strategy? One perfectly acceptable way would be to formulaically reduce your equity allocation as a function of your age. Say by age 40 you've figured out that you're comfortable with a 70/30 stock and bond mix. You might decide that by age 70 you want to be no more than 25/75. This entails lowering your equity allocation by 1.5% each year between ages 40 and 70. Yet another way would involve a gradual switch from a bond fund to a TIPS ladder, as detailed by Michael Zwecher in his book, *Retirement Portfolios*.[11]

Markets fluctuate, so I suggest another path. If, at any point, a bull market pushes your portfolio over the LMP "magic number" of 25 times your RLE, you've won the investing game. Why keep playing? Start getting out. After you've put enough TIPS, plain-vanilla Treasuries, and CDs into your mental LMP, you're free to start buying risky assets again. If stocks continue their rise, you can slowly transfer even more assets into a separate low-risk pool earmarked for emergencies, risky asset equity purchases at lower prices, and nice-to-have luxuries.

As you might expect, just when this critical transition comes — or even if it comes — depends on the interplay of three factors: your savings rate, your asset allocation, and, critically, the whims of the market gods. There's no way of predicting the event, but in order to get some sense of the urgency with which the saver should begin transitioning from risky assets to riskless ones — even if the amount is significantly less than the LMP — I created a mythical soon-to-be retiree named Samantha Saver who was able to put 20% of her salary each year into the S&P 500 and whose Social Security and pensions will meet 30% of her retirement income needs. Samantha's total retirement needs are, as with the previous examples, 25 years of living expenses, which comes out to 20 years of salary (since she needed only 80% of that salary to live on). After the 30% of her living expenses from Social Security and pensions are factored in, her needs decrease to just 14 years of salary. Next, I've placed Samantha in a theoretical world in which her aggressive portfolio earns a real 4% each and every year. Assuming that she begins work at age 25, she'll reach her goal after 34 years, at age 59, at which time she tucks her LMP baseball safely in her purse and goes home. Figure 4-8 charts her happy theoretical savings career.

Now, let's throw a monkey wrench into her plans by tossing the sequence of post-1929 stock returns at her at various times. For illustrative purposes, Figure 4-9 shows what happens if the

Figure 4-8
Samantha Saver Paradigm

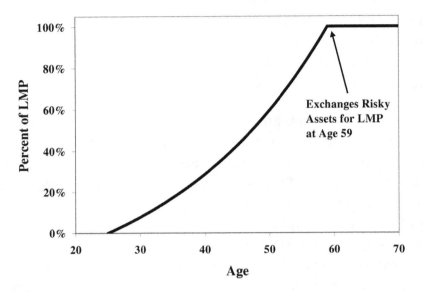

Figure 4-9
Samantha Saver Depression Paradigm

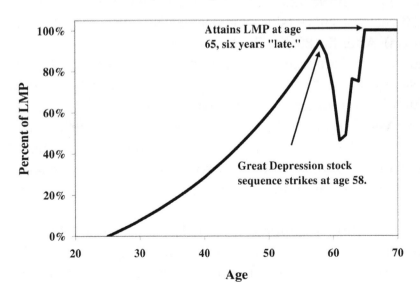

post-1929 real stock returns series strikes her portfolio at age 58, one year before she would have otherwise hit her LMP.

Table 4-2. Samantha Saver, Scenarios: Effect of Post-1929 Real Stock Returns Beginning at Ages before She Reaches LMP at Age 59

Age post-1929 real returns strike Samantha's portfolio	Age Samantha reaches LMP
Does not	59
58	65
57	64
56	64
55	63
54	62
53	61
52	60
51	59
50	58
49	65
48	65
47	65
46	64
45	63
44	62
43	61
42	60
41	59
40	63
39	62
38	61
37	60
36	59

Samantha's portfolio takes a big hit, but because of the purchases made in 1930 to 1932 and the subsequent recovery, she does reach her LMP at age 65—6 years late. Table 4-2 repeats this exercise by hitting her portfolio at progressively earlier years, to illustrate exactly how this sequence affected her LMP date.

What's interesting about Table 4-2 is that no matter what year the post-1929 stock disaster—which produced a 1.37% real annualized return over the next 20 years—struck Samantha, it doesn't drastically affect the age at which she reached her LMP. Perhaps she really wanted to retire at age 59, but during the Great Depression years having to wait until 65 to retire would not have struck most people as a hardship.

More important, Table 4-2 tells us precious little about when to convert the nest egg into a more conservative LMP-like portfolio. In fact, this exercise may even suggest that it doesn't matter that much exactly when it's done, *as long as it's done more than a few years before you retire*—as delineated earlier in this chapter by Sam Sixty-Five's disastrous experience. The big difference between the outcomes of Samantha and Sam is that Samantha's continuing stream of savings, even late in her working career, gave her the option of working a little longer to both build capital and enjoy the recovery in stock prices, and so ensure her retirement. For Sam, that particular cavalry could not come and save him from an impoverished old age.

Let's get back to basics. The Nalebuff-Ayres model has a life-cycle stock exposure that typically holds maximal leverage until about age 30, followed by a rapid decline in equity exposure, which falls below 100% around age 45 and then continues downward to very low levels in retirement. The more conventional "rule of 110" (stock exposure = 110 minus age) is, overall, more conservative. Both were plotted in Figure 4-4. The key point of this section is that the conversion from an aggressive accumulation-phase portfolio to a risk-free LMP doesn't have to be an all-at-once phenomenon. If, for example, you're actually able to tolerate an aggressive, 100% factor-loaded equity portfolio at age 45 and are well on your way to a full LMP-sized nest egg by 65, then the slope of that lessening of stock exposure is 5% per year. In a year with high equity returns, you might drop your equity exposure by 10%, but in a year with low or negative returns, you might not lower your equity exposure at all.

In the final analysis, the decision of when to convert some or all of your nest egg to an LMP relates to your risk tolerance. Those who are highly risk averse will probably do so as soon as their portfolio reaches LMP size, allowing them the luxury of sleeping soundly through the night. Others may be willing to take some risk for a shot at the further potential rewards of risky assets—business-class travel, extravagant gifts to grandchildren, or an earlier retirement. If you want to know when to convert your risky savings to your LMP, you'll have to know who you are.

Life after the LMP

If you're especially lucky or hard-working, you're not going to stop saving when you reach your LMP. What's beyond the LMP? The RP, the risk portfolio. While you might daydream about splashing out for a Beemer or jumping aboard the Orient Express for a jaunt to Venice, the mere fact that you're reading this book suggests that your grandkids' college needs and your own philanthropic aspirations likely rank higher on your list than your own current consumption. In other words, you may not be managing the RP for yourself.

Then again, if your RP grows large enough, it may completely absorb your LMP. Recall that during the Great Depression real dividends fell temporarily by only half. Since the dividend yield of the U.S. stock market is currently around 2%, and since even during the Great Depression the real payout did not fall by more than half, you can count on spending one-half of this dollar amount—that is, 1% of the value of your stocks.

Can you accumulate 100 years of RLE? In the first place, as already pointed out, if you have enough in Social Security and pensions, you may not even need an LMP. Even so, relatively few are so fortunate. And even if you are, you'll need a trait that is even less common: an ability to tolerate a 100% stock portfolio through the thick and thin. The joint probability of those two factors—a nest egg that is 100 times larger than RLE and the ability to withstand an all-equity portfolio—is vanishingly small.

How risky should the RP be? As risky as you can tolerate. By the time you've filled out your LMP, you should have a pretty good idea of your risk tolerance. Behavioral finance research clearly shows that investors are more daring with profits than with original capital—the so-called house money effect—and this description fits the RP well enough.[12]

What If I Never Get There?

The Samantha Saver model described earlier in this chapter—a savings of 20% of salary invested in a risky portfolio with a 4% real return, which converted to an LMP that provided 25 years of RLE at age 59—makes for a good reality check on how well you're doing. Five years before she retired, Samantha had accumulated 19 years of RLE. Ten years before, she had 14. Fifteen years before, she had 10, and 20 before, she had 6.5.

If you're significantly behind this schedule, then you have a problem—a big one, in fact. There are only three choices in this situation:

- Take more risk.
- Work longer and/or work part time in retirement.
- Lower your standard of living in retirement.

The first choice—taking more risk—is no choice at all. You're skydiving, but in place of a parachute you have only sweaty palms. You'll almost certainly screw it up. Don't do it.

Your best bet is some combination of belt tightening and postponement of retirement, after which you'll still work part time. And on that happy note, we'll tie up some loose ends, and then proceed to get our fingers dirty with the vehicles that, with luck, will get us to, and beyond, our LMP.

CHAPTER 5

LOOSE ENDS

Astute readers of this book have noticed by now that I've eliminated some material covered in my previous wide-angle investment tomes, in particular, market history and the impact of the investment business on the individual investor. That's because, as you're tired of hearing by now, I've assumed that you're an investing adult and already conversant with these subjects. Nonetheless, there are some new things worthy of discussion.

The New Normal: Electronic Bolts from the Blue

You're well aware of stories of the Tulipmania of the 1630s, the diving company bubble of the 1690s, the South Sea/Mississippi companies of 1719 and 1720, and the railway mania of the 1840s. Plus, you have firsthand experience of the game-changing events of recent financial history—from the euphoric heights of the 1990s tech bubble to the dismal depths of the 2008–2009 global financial crisis. What's new is the chaos wrought by computerized markets. At the time of this writing, more than 70% of trading is algorithmic. That means that about half of all transactions are done by superfast computers *trading with each other*.[1]

Leaving aside the trade-off between improved liquidity and investor confidence wrought by high-speed trading, these systems have introduced a new form of instability into the securities markets. In the past, the close observer kept an eye out for the signs of market froth: the relative joining her first investment club or the television advertisements featuring a guy who just bought his own island—modern versions, in other words, of Joseph Kennedy's proverbial bootblack dispensing stock market advice.

Now, there's a new wild card present in the securities markets, what author Richard Bookstaber calls "a demon of our own design."[2] These are the securities markets version of Charles Perrow's "normal accidents" paradigm: disasters that occur simply because a system is too complex for humans to understand and whose moving parts are so tightly coupled that deviations from normal operation occur too rapidly to contain.[3] The nuclear reactor accidents at Three Mile Island, Chernobyl, and Fukushima are classic cases. Modern securities markets fit this model to a tee.

Take May 6, 2010 as an example. At 2:32 p.m. eastern daylight time on that date, a market participant, cryptically identified later in an SEC report as a "large Fundamental Seller (a mutual fund complex)," initiated a sell order of approximately $4.1 billion of the E-Mini S&P 500 futures. Critically, the algorithm chosen did what no sane human trader would have done: feed these sales into the market over a matter of minutes, without regard to price. This initiated a cascade of events that caused the

Dow to plummet by some 1,000 points, followed by an almost complete recovery, all in the space of several minutes.[4] Shaken investors drove the broad market down by about 10% over the next several weeks.

Although the stock exchanges adjusted their procedures to require appropriate human input in such circumstances, complex linked systems, by their very nature, harbor myriad unknown failure modes. We face a future of repeated, spasmodic, and, at times, violent, market drops, each with a different trigger and course. To compound the damage, these plunges will come straight out of nowhere. There won't be any uninformed relatives, outrageous advertisements, or bootblacks to warn you.

Such random and severe turbulence may offer more opportunity than danger in the long run. It's just one more reason to maintain adequate reserves of patience, cash, and courage. But our financial system has grown so large and complex that the damage may occasionally spill over from Wall Street to Main Street.

The Duration of Bonds—and Stocks

Duration is an important dimension of the risk of a fixed-income portfolio. (For now, we'll ignore the other important dimension, credit risk, the probability of default.) The classic definition of duration is both intuitively twisted and practically useless: the dollar-weighted average of the time elapsed by the cash flows from interest and principal, each discounted by the bond's interest rate. Since the biggest of these, by far, is usually the principal payment, duration is always somewhat less than the maturity, and the gap between duration and maturity grows with both higher interest rates and longer maturities. For example, the duration of the current 10-year Treasury bond yielding 2.8% is 8.8 years. If the interest rate were 10%, the duration would shorten to 6.5 years.

There are two far more intuitive definitions of duration. The first is that duration closely approximates the ratio between interest rate rise and price fall. Thus, if you just bought the 10-year bond at 2.8% and yields rose to 3.8%, your bond is now worth approximately 8.8% less. (In other words, not as bad as what happened in 2013 when the 10-year note yield rose from 1.66% to 2.98%.)

A second, and even more useful, definition of duration is the break-even point resulting from reinvesting interest payments at the higher coupon. If, for example, you've just bought the 2.8% 10-year note and interest rates rise to 3.8%, the 8.8% capital loss would be repaired by the fact that you're now getting an extra percent of interest on interest. At 8.8 years, you'll have exactly the same amount of *nominal* discounted capital as if interest rates had remained at 2.8%. (Of course, that kind of interest rate rise is often the result of unexpected inflation, in which case you definitely are worse off by that point.)

The extent to which you're saving and investing functionally shortens the break-even duration point. If you're a young person who had just begun accumulating 10-year notes when the rate rose by 1%, then your effective portfolio duration is very short indeed, perhaps only a few months. To the extent that your nest egg begins to dwarf your savings, the break-even duration lengthens appropriately. Were you a retiree who is no longer saving, you'd be hit with the full effective 8.8 year duration of your loss.

Stocks, of course, have a duration, too. For example, they are currently yielding about 2.0%. If they decline 75% in price and the absolute amount of the dividend remains the same, you are now investing those dividends at a yield that is four times higher, 8%, at which rate you can purchase much cheaper shares. Eventually, this will redound to your benefit, and you will wind up better off than at the lower yield/higher price. How long does it take to catch up? That depends on the beginning yield and the magnitude of the decline. This model shows that with today's 2.0% stock yield, a 25% decline would have a duration of 62 years, a 50% decline 50 years, a 75% decline 33 years, and a 90% decline only 19 years.

Skeptics will point out that a 90% stock decline would likely be associated with a decrease in the absolute dividend amount, but as already mentioned, the real dividend stream of the Dow during the Great Depression decreased by only about 50%, and only temporarily. In fact, the 1929–1933 bear market provides a superb reality check of the above model. One nominal dollar invested in stocks on August 29, 1929 declined in value to 16.6 cents by July 1, 1932 and rose back to par by the end of January 1945, less than 13 years after the bottom.

The dividend yield was 2.6% in September 1929. For the 30 years after that earnings growth was only 1.8%. Had the Crash not occurred, stocks would have returned a real 4.4% per year, resulting in a "break-even" point with what actually occurred in January 1952, or 22 years, close to the 19-year period predicted by the duration model. Viewed from this perspective, the market today is even more frightening than it was in 1929 for the simple reason that a lower starting dividend yield (recall that it's 2% today) produces a longer duration. Certainly, such a wrenching market decline today would wreak havoc on the financial and social structure of the country, as it did 70 years ago. Put another way, today's high prices and resultant low yields are no great blessing.

As with bonds, the young saver can effectively decrease the break-even duration point of stocks to almost nothing—that is, she can eliminate risk—to the extent that she has human capital and future savings greatly in excess of her retirement portfolio.

This reinforces the point made in chapter 4. It makes little sense to discuss the riskiness of stocks without specifying the ratio of human capital to investment capital. The lower that ratio is, the higher the risk. All investors should avoid nonsystemic risk— that is, the risks of not being properly diversified. But, to the extent that they can stomach it, younger savers, at least, should embrace as much systemic market risk as they can.

The Ben Bernanke Blues

Low nominal and real interest rates are the pits. Whether you're trying to fund your LMP with TIPS or are just plain miserable with the near-zero return on your liquid assets, very few people are happy with the so-called "financial repression" foisted on investors by the world's accommodative central bankers in the wake of the GFC.

Well, cheer up. It's better than you think. I have in my mind the image of Ben Bernanke and Mario Draghi aiming garden hoses at a bucket, about 20 yards away, that represents the world economy, and they're slowly filling it up with, um, liquidity. Their aim is poor, so much of the water is splashing on the lawn on which the bucket sits, that lawn being risky assets of all types: stocks, real estate, and, increasingly and ominously, real estate loans on increasingly dodgy properties, particularly in China and other developing nations.

But in plain English (at least as of this writing) you have more assets than you deserve. Had Messrs. Bernanke and Draghi *not* opened up with the hoses, your portfolios would be worth less—likely, a lot less.

Consider the following small thought experiment. Imagine that you're a recently retired 65 year-old who plans to be pushing up the daisies in exactly 30 years and that your real RLE throughout that period will be $50,000. Let's further assume that you're going to be funding your first year's expenses with $50,000 in cash on January 1 of that year. In each successive year, you'll do the same with an inflation-adjusted $50,000 from a maturing TIPS until you reach your 94th birthday. At that point you will set your mortality alarm for 365 days. (Never mind that there are no TIPS maturing on January 1, or for that matter, between 2032 and 2040.)

If you discount each future year's real $50,000 by $(1 + r)^n$, where r is the TIPS yield in year n and n ranges from 1 to 29 years in the future, and if we plug in each year's TIPS yield as of November 26, 2013, then we come up with a present value of $1,298,842 needed to purchase this particular LMP. (It's no coincidence that this is 26 years of real RLE, close enough to the 25 times real RLE that I've assumed for the LMP.)

Now, let's assume that in a "normal" counterfactual world, the TIPS yield is 2.0% at all maturities. In this case, we find that our TIPS LMP costs only $1,142,219. In other words, because of the Fed's accommodative policy, it costs 13.7% more to retire ($1,298,842 compared to $1,142,842). It's a lead-pipe cinch that unless you've been investing your retirement nest egg almost exclusively in T-bills and CDs since the GFC (And since you're an investing adult, you'd never do anything that dumb, right?), the Bernanke Factor has been worth a good deal more than 13.7% to your portfolio.

So rejoice. You're sitting pretty, and the lousy present yields are a small price to pay for a pleasantly bloated portfolio—at least as of this moment.

Beware of Geeks (and BRICs) Bearing Gifts

You're an investing adult, so you know that glamorous, rapidly growing companies have, in general, *lower* returns than doggy value stocks. But many investing adults, including some of the most respected names in academic finance, make a nearly identical erroneous connection: that between rapidly growing economies and supposedly high returns on securities.

The Chinese stock market is the poster child for this phenomenon. Over the past few decades, its economy has been growing at double-digit rates, but over the nearly 21 years from January 1993 through the end of October 2013, the U.S. dollar total return of the MSCI large+mid-cap index was exactly 2.77%—that is, about 0.13% annualized in nominal terms, or a -2.24% real annualized return.

The gross disproportion between China's economic growth and its equity returns raises fundamental questions about the nature of its securities markets and of Chinese society in general. For example, the 50 wealthiest U.S. congressmen have a collective net worth of about $1.6 billion. That's nothing to sneeze at, but that average net worth (about $33 million) of those representatives places them nowhere near the apex of American wealth. That space is mostly occupied by entrepreneurs and financial types. By contrast, the 50 wealthiest members of the Chinese National People's Congress have a combined net worth of $95 billion.[5] Such rampant corruption is hardly the exception in developing markets.

China's corruption hearkens back to the Crédit Mobilier episode of 1872. In that scandal, numerous congressmen, as well as both of Ulysses Grant's vice presidents, received sweetheart deals on the purchase price of shares in Crédit Mobilier, a construction company formed and secretly owned by shareholders of the Union Pacific Railroad, which had contracted with the federal government to build part of the transcontinental railroad. In a complex fraud, Union Pacific was able to conceal from public view the railroad's inflated construction costs when, in fact, both Union Pacific and Crédit Mobilier had identical managements. Like water flowing by gravity, the excess millions in profit eventually made their way to the well-positioned Crédit Mobilier and Union Pacific shareholders.

In both today's China and 1872's Crédit Mobilier scandal, a good portion of the dirty money was channeled through newly created shares. By one estimate, China's equity pool is diluted with new shares to the tune of about 30% per year, many of which likely find their way into the hands of government officials.[6]

Let's assume that for the past 20 years China's economy has been growing at a real rate of 10% per year and that aggregate corporate profits have been growing along with them at about the same rate. If the share pool is growing faster than 10%, then *per-share* earnings have been falling. This goes a long way towards explaining the poor performance of Chinese equity.

While the data and math surrounding Chinese equity dilution may be muddy, the history of developed markets provides a clearer picture of the interaction among GDP growth, aggregate profits, and per-share earnings and dividend growth.

The United States has a very long GDP series indeed, extending back over 200 years. It turns out that the American economy has averaged 3% growth per year, adjusted for inflation (with roughly 2% coming from productivity growth and 1% from population growth). The 2% growth slope in productivity, (which closely tracks per-capita GDP) seems to be something of a macroeconomic constant, seen in most advanced economies. (Developing nations can experience much higher "catch-up" growth, but this eventually slows down as these nations approach "developed" status.) So far, so good.

Does this translate into a similar growth of aggregate corporate profits? Indeed, it does! Since 1929, when the predecessors of the Bureau of Economic Analysis started keeping track, corporate profits have been about 10% of GDP, which is the "classical" share of capital in a "normal" economy. Traditionally, labor gets around 80%, and land (rents), the remaining 10%. Of late, however, increasing income disparity seems to be driving up capital's share at the expense of labor. That gap is more properly the realm of a book on sociology and politics, so we'll avoid the subject except to note that over the long run, profits cannot grow at a rate greater than the economy, since it will eventually hit the upper bound of 100%. That, of course, is a theoretical bound, since long before it is reached, the proles will have stormed the ramparts.

Having established that corporate profits track GDP, we'll zoom out again with the historical lens. There are reasonably good data going back almost to the birth of the republic on corporate dividends and from 1871 on corporate earnings. These data show that the growth of both per-share earnings and dividends is not much more than 1% per year. The DMS database shows that in most developed nations, per-share real dividend growth is also this low. In more than a few nations, it's actually negative.

This difference between GDP growth and dividend/earnings growth is, of course, caused by the dilution of stock shares, which in the U.S. seems to run at about 2% per year. The same 2% gap has also been observed in the world's most stable developed economies. Less fortunate nations that were devastated during the twentieth century's wars (Germany, Japan, Italy, France, and Spain) saw about 4% dilution of shares, which was brought on by the recapitalization of their damaged industrial base. (Rob Arnott and I independently confirmed this 2% dilution rate in the U.S. by comparing the different rates of growth of the price and capitalization indexes of the all-market CRSP 1-10 index. Between 1926 and 2000, the number of shares traded in the U.S. stock market grew by roughly a factor of five.)[7]

To complete the picture, Larry Speidell and his colleagues used the same algorithm to determine that share dilution, while very high in Asia's emerging stock markets, was, paradoxically, very low in Latin America's stock markets.[8] This is reflected in the returns of stocks in these two regions. Between January 1988 and October 2013, the MSCI-Latin America Index returned an annualized 18.37%. In contrast, the MSCI Emerging Markets Asia Index returned 8.29% (and the S&P 500, 10.34%).

Most people would find it hard to believe that Asia's red-hot economies would result in equity returns that were a full 10% per year lower than in Latin America. But such is the irrefutable logic of equity returns in developing markets, where "rapidly growing" most often means "more rapidly diluting."

What Color Is Your Risk?

Now that we've fleshed out our portfolio goals and design more fully, we'll need to explore the concept of "risk" in a more nuanced fashion. In chapter 1, we settled on Antti Ilmanen's definition of risk as "bad returns in bad times."

This served us well for individual assets, but you don't own individual assets. You own a portfolio, whose goal is meeting future consumption needs. Risk, at the portfolio level, is not a statistical measure. It is, rather, the probability that you will fail to meet your future needs—in plain English, that you might run out of money and die poor.

Let's start with a Rip Van Winkle retiree who has accumulated a small nest egg and who intends to sleep for 114 years, then wake up and retire. Why 114 years? That's the length of the best information we have on worldwide securities returns, the DMS database, which now extends from 1900 to 2013.⁹ Table 5-1 summarizes the DMS results. Two things from this table fairly leap off the page. First, over the long run, in every single nation studied, stocks returned more than bonds, and almost always by a large margin, while bonds outperformed bills by a smaller margin. Second, although the return on stocks in many nations was low, a globally diversified, market-cap-weighted approach did very well indeed—again, much better than a global fixed-income portfolio.

Table 5-1 demonstrates, as clearly as any data can, that over very long time periods, risk and return become the same thing. Moreover, from a very long-term, consumption-based perspective, stocks are much more likely to meet your consumption needs than bonds or bills simply because stocks have such a relatively high return.

Note also that Table 5-1 reflects the awful inflation that was so pervasive in the twentieth century. In the wake of both world wars, almost every nation, other than Switzerland and the Netherlands, was touched by it to some degree.

Table 5-1. Real Returns of Stocks, Bonds, and Bills, 1900–2013

Nation	Real stock return	Real bond return	Real bill return
Australia	7.4%	1.5%	0.7%
Austria	0.7%	-4.1%	-8.1%
Belgium	2.6%	0.2%	-0.3%
Canada	5.7%	2.1%	1.5%

Table 5-1. Continued

Denmark	5.2%	3.1%	2.1%
Finland	5.8%	0.0%	-0.5%
France	3.2%	0.0%	-2.8%
Germany	3.2%	-1.6%*	-2.4%*
Ireland	4.1%	1.4%	0.7%
Italy	1.9%	-1.5%	-3.6%
Japan	4.1%	-0.9%	-1.9%
Netherlands	4.9%	1.5%	0.6%
New Zealand	6.0%	2.0%	1.7%
Norway	4.3%	1.8%	1.1%
Portugal	3.7%	0.6%	-1.1%
South Africa	7.4%	1.8%	1.0%
Spain	3.6%	1.4%	0.3%
Sweden	5.8%	2.6%	1.9%
Switzerland	4.4%	2.2%	0.8%
United Kingdom	5.3%	1.4%	0.9%
United States	6.5%	1.9%	0.9%
World (cap weighted)	5.2%	1.8%	0.9%

Data source: Elroy Dimson, Paul Marsh, Mike Staunton, *Credit Suisse Global Investment Returns Yearbook 2013*.

*Includes break during inflation of 1922–1923. Many bonds and mortgages, which had zero real value, were eventually partially reimbursed in real terms. See Costantino Bresciani-Turroni, Millicent E. Sayers, trans., *The Economics of Inflation* (Northhampton, UK: John Dickens & Co. Ltd., 1937) 321–25.

Stocks do suffer in the first stages of inflation—that is, from *unexpected* inflation. But as an economy accommodates itself to constantly rising prices, stocks are a pretty good hedge against them in the long run. The easiest way to think about this is to recall that Japanese and German bondholders saw losses of more than 95% during and immediately after the Second World War. Over the same period, stocks in both nations fell by about 90%. Bondholders held what were, in most cases, nearly worthless pieces of paper that never regained their real value, while stockholders owned claims on the assets of the likes of Siemens, Daimler, Bayer, and Mitsubishi. When recapitalized and rebuilt, these companies regained their real prewar value in less than a decade in Germany and in about 15 years in Japan. During the twentieth century, Belgium, Finland, France, and Italy showed the same pattern of severe permanent real capital loss of fixed-income assets, with the subsequent recovery of equity real capital wealth. In the wake of *two* world wars, Germany, of course, experienced this pattern twice.[10]

French markets present a typical picture of this unfortunate inflationary group. In the 40 years between 1940 and 1979, French investors saw the real value of their bills fall by 96% (-7.8% annualized) and of their bonds by 84% (-4.5% annualized). French stocks (with dividends reinvested) were hardly on fire, but their real value actually increased by 124% (2.0% annualized).[11]

Even more spectacular was Chile's performance. Over the 70 years between 1927 and 1996, it experienced 33.16% annualized inflation, enough to produce a 508-million-fold rise in prices. Yet its stock market brought real returns of 7% to 8% per year, better than the stock market in the United States. Similarly, over the 40 years between 1957 and 1996, Israel had 33.02% yearly inflation, with nearly identically high stock returns.[12]

Thus, if the twentieth century is any guide to the very long run, bondholders of developed nations can expect to suffer permanent capital loss that equity holders will avoid. In Keynes' famous phrase, "euthanasia of the rentier," indeed.[13]

In a previous publication, I defined "deep risk" as a *permanent* loss of inflation-adjusted capital, from which there is no recovery, over the course of an investor's lifetime.[14] According to that formulation, then, even the 2008–2009 and 1929–1932 bear markets did not constitute deep risk, since the real value of stocks repaired themselves within about 4 years and 10 years, respectively.

Are there other sources of deep risk beyond inflation? Theoretically, there are at least three others: deflation, confiscation (by the government, either by outright seizure or through very high tax rates), and devastation (from war, either localized or worldwide). In the fiat money world, outright deflation is relatively uncommon, and your options for dealing with confiscation and devastation are very limited. Thus, you should focus your attention on the deep risk of inflation. It is the most likely threat you'll face, and it's the one risk you can do the most about.

The problem, of course, is that, endowments aside, none of us has 114 years to invest. The history of markets, on the other hand, demonstrates that over short time periods, we do have to worry about "shallow" risk (that is, temporary risk, no matter how severe). Further, since humans experience risk as a short-term phenomenon (remember from chapter 1 the yellow and black stripes of the tiger in your peripheral vision), shallow risk is the one most of us think of when we use that fraught four-letter word.

Where is the borderland between shallow and deep risk? To answer this, recall the point made repeatedly in this book: how "risky" stocks are depends mainly on the stage of an investor's life cycle. For the young saver, as we've already discussed, a turbulent market with long-run low returns (allowing her to buy large numbers of shares at low prices) is a deliverance devoutly to be wished. At the other end of the spectrum, a high-volatility/ low-return market can give a retiree's nest egg the deep six faster than you can say "financial crisis." The key variable, then, is the ratio of human capital to investment capital. The transition between deep and shallow risk thus occurs at approximately the point where human capital and investment capital are equal. For most individuals, this occurs a bit after the midpoint of the working career, at age 45 or 50. (The one exception to this rule is the very young trustafarian with a large amount of assets that he or she won't need for at least a few decades.)

Before this transition point, the investor with more human capital than investment capital (or a young one with a lot of assets) is concerned mainly with the "deep risks" I've listed above and should, thus, have a fairly aggressive portfolio.

Once the amount of investment capital greatly exceeds the human capital, which for most people, if they're lucky enough, occurs just before retirement, shallow risk, which is best protected against by high-quality fixed-income assets, especially

TIPS, comes to the fore for those assets needed to defray future retirement expenses, the LMP.

As we've discussed, the ticklish part of the process occurs as one makes the transition from an investment strategy focused on deep risk to one focused on shallow risk. That's the point at which one starts to convert to an LMP the risky part of the portfolio that has grown to sufficient size to retire on, and takes it off the table.

In chapter 6, we'll discuss, in general terms, how to design portfolios with these goals in mind.

CHAPTER 6

WALKING THE WALK: NUTS AND BOLTS FOR INVESTING ADULTS

You're an investing adult, so you already know how to deploy your portfolio into a mix of stock and fixed-income assets as described in chapter 2—that is, as passively as possible and appropriately tilted towards value, growth, momentum, and profitability.

As such, I'll make some final comments on how to execute these strategies in the current investing environment. For those who want model portfolios, I'll sketch some out.

To ETF or Not to ETF

A persistent criticism levied against my books is that they're "outdated" because I ignore ETFs. Guilty as charged: I *do* pretty much ignore them, but not because there's anything wrong with the ETF wrapper. Like open-end funds, there are good ones and there are bad ones. It's just that a wrapper is, well, just that. As with most products, the wrapping doesn't make a difference to the intelligent consumer. It's what's inside that counts.

I'll take that one step further. Anyone who tells you that there is something magical about ETFs that makes them significantly better than open-end funds in the same asset class is blowing a large amount of an aerosolized sooty particulate cloud. In most cases, whether you use an ETF or open-end fund makes exactly zero difference. Consider this: Over the objections of founder John Bogle, Vanguard now offers an ETF class of virtually all of its open-end index funds. These ETFs carry the same expense ratio as the Admiral class mutual funds, invest in the same underlying pool of assets, have the same tax efficiency, and, therefore, have nearly identical returns in almost all cases. It cannot be any other way.

There are certain circumstances where the chosen wrapper does make a difference, the most important area being bonds. I highly recommend that you avoid *all* ETF bond funds. To understand why, I'll need to explain some of the trading mechanics involved. An ETF, unlike an open-end fund, trades throughout the day at a discount or premium relative to the net asset value (NAV) of the underlying shares. In most cases, the spread between the two is minimal because shares are both created and liquidated by independent agents: "authorized participants" (AP) who buy up the securities underlying the funds and bundle them into ETF shares that are then delivered to the fund company. The same process also works in reverse to liquidate ETF shares. Were a significant spread to open up between the market price and NAV, the AP, in theory, should simply arbitrage that away at a profit.

This mechanism works well with stocks, which are highly liquid, but not with bonds, which are not. There is, for example, only one commonly traded class of Ford Motor Company stock. By contrast, Ford has a range of bonds of varying issue dates, coupons, and maturities. Since there are so many more individual bonds than stocks, the bonds can be highly illiquid. During a financial disturbance, when liquidity becomes even thinner and most corporate bonds trade only "by appointment," the AP mechanism fails, often at considerable disadvantage to the shareholder. The open-end fund holder, who can always buy and sell at the 4 p.m. (eastern standard time) NAV, has no such problem.

For the lion's share of your fixed-income assets, the entire mutual fund structure is, in fact, unnecessary. To repeat this book's opening mantra: there are risky assets, and there are riskless ones, and the two play very different roles. Keep the two as separate as possible and make the risky assets as risky as you like. Critically, your riskless assets should retain their value in a crisis. Corporate bonds, in particular, have a modest amount of stock-like behavior and can see price falls independent of the rise or fall in overall interest rates.

Municipal bonds can also behave this way, and if you're depending on either corporates or munis for liquidity during a crisis—precisely when you're likely to want or need it the most—you may have to take a substantial haircut to realize it. Tax-sheltered investors should keep almost all of their fixed-income assets in government-guaranteed securities: Treasury bills and notes and CDs. And while taxable investors should own at least some municipal bonds, they should still hold a fair dollop of Treasuries and CDs, as well. The main point here is that you don't need or want to own a mutual fund for Treasuries, and it's neither desirable nor available for CDs.

When purchasing CDs, you will need to keep an eye on the FDIC's insured limit of $250,000 per person per institution (though a good bank manager can get fairly creative in extending this limit by varying ownership and beneficiary designations). They can also be bought from a brokerage account, which has the advantage of convenience and immediate access, especially at maturity, when they simply roll into the cash/money-market balance. On the other hand, CDs sold by a brokerage can impose a haircut of principal if they are sold before maturity, whereas usually only a limited interest penalty is incurred when you redeem before maturity at the issuing bank. If you're especially clever and aggressive, it is often better to buy a higher-coupon, longer-maturity CD directly from the bank. If sold before maturity, the extra coupon will usually more than make up for the interest penalty. Don't try this at a brokerage.

Unless your account size is tiny, it makes *no* sense to own a Treasury or government-bond fund, since you can buy these securities at auction and hold them at no cost. The same goes double for TIPS, the main purpose of which is to pay for future real living expenses. You can, with a little effort, tailor a ladder to do so with the proceeds as they mature. If, on the other hand, you hold a TIPS fund, not only do you pay unnecessary fund fees, but there will likely be periods when you will be forced to sell these securities at disadvantageous prices, as happened to many investors in 2008–2009. Much as I love Vanguard's low fees, there's almost no reason to pay them even a penny for their TIPS and government-bond funds. Except for the smallest of portfolios, the same is largely true for bond index funds. Their largest holdings are government securities, but they also mix in a fair amount of riskier (i.e., stock-like) corporate bonds of lower quality.

The only bond funds you should own are open-end municipal and corporate bond funds (to the extent that you do own these two asset classes). The reason for this is simple. Without a great deal of effort and expense, the individual cannot put together a well-diversified low-expense mix of municipal or corporate securities. With munis, the choice is clear: Vanguard offers a wide variety of national and state-specific mutual funds.

Corporate bond funds are curiously problematic. For many years, Vanguard maintained a "corporate bond fund" series, which then inexplicably changed both its name (to the "investment grade" appellation) and its mandate, which was broadened to include government as well as asset-backed (credit card and car loans) and mortgage-backed securities. Although these funds have good long-term records, they proved especially vexing during the Global Financial Crisis—a classic case of "bad returns in bad times." In 2008, the Intermediate Investment Grade Bond Fund, for example, lost 6.06%, versus a loss of 2.76% for the equivalent Barclays Intermediate Credit (corporate) Index, a remarkable showing considering that the fund held a significant amount of government bonds, which did well in the crisis. To be frank, I simply do not trust the management of this fund series. Even more remarkable, Vanguard has recently brought out, hooray, a series of corporate-bond index funds. Unfortunately, the intermediate- and long-term open-end versions of these funds come with purchase fees (0.25% and 1.00%, respectively). Only the short-term version Admiral Class shares come with no fee. (All 3 funds come as fee-less ETFs, but, as I've explained above, I do not recommend bond ETFs.)

A reasonable fixed-income allocation for a largely sheltered portfolio might be equal amounts of CDs and Treasury bills or notes. A largely taxable portfolio might be equal parts munis, CDs, and Treasuries.

To ETF or Not to ETF—Stocks

I have no problems—none at all—with stock ETFs from the major providers of plain-vanilla total-market/cap-weighted and tilted products: Vanguard, iShares, and Powershares. Be warned that you should probably only consider funds with more than $200 million in assets. Anything under that amount puts their survival at risk.

As mentioned in the Introduction, since you're an investing adult, I'm not going to provide a plethora of detailed model portfolios containing specific stock and bond fund allocations. Rather, I'll supply guidelines about overall strategy. I'm also going to assume that you know how to do the basic sort of four-function math necessary to adjust stock allocations up and down with varying risk exposure. In the long run it makes almost no difference whether you use the Fidelity Spartan Total Market Index Fund or the Vanguard Large-Cap ETF for your U.S. large market exposure—although the former is a total-market fund and the latter is not. For much the same reason, it makes little long-run difference if you use the Dimensional (DFA) U.S. Small-Cap Value Portfolio or the PowerShares FTSE RAFI US 1500 Small-Mid Portfolio for your domestic small value exposure (if, in fact, you feel the need to own that asset class).

For the investing adult who wants a simple 15-minute-a-year market-cap-weighted portfolio that frees them up to pursue a career, enjoy the kids and grandkids, and get on with life, you can't do better than to use total market index funds for both domestic and foreign exposure (including emerging markets). I recommend Vanguard's products, since both its domestic and international offerings contain small and midsize company shares. If you can make the $10,000 minimum purchase of the Admiral class shares, I prefer them to the ETF class. But if you want to buy the ETFs for these two, be my guest. And if you want to keep things really simple and not own CDs and individual Treasuries, feel free to ignore my dislike of bond index funds and deploy a classic "three-fund portfolio": a total domestic stock fund, a total international stock fund, and a bond index fund. (At present, very low rates might make you consider using the appropriate share class of the Short-Term Bond Index Fund, rather than the more "traditional" Total Bond Market Index Fund.) And, to reiterate, I would own an open-end bond index fund, not a bond ETF. Given that foreign stocks are a bit cheaper than U.S. stocks in early 2014, a 60/40 mix of U.S./foreign equity seems appropriate.

If you want to tilt towards other return factors, such as small, value, momentum, and profitability, my go-to fund company has been and remains Dimensional Fund Advisors. Their funds tend to be more heavily exposed to these tilts, and their fund managers have maintained their funds' asset-class purities with rigor. They cleanly exclude REITs, for example, from their equity portfolios, which other index fund providers, including Vanguard, iShares, and Powershares, do not. This allows more precise control of your exposure to this diversifying asset class, especially the segregation of REITs into the tax-sheltered part of your portfolio, where they belong. Their tilted foreign and domestic products are probably not as tax-efficient as ETFs in the same asset classes, but this is more than offset by the lower factor loading of the ETFs.

A word or two about DFA access, which almost always requires that you use an investment advisor. First, investing adulthood and paying for an investment advisor are not mutually exclusive. Many sophisticated investors use an advisor because they're extremely busy with their day jobs or appreciate the emotional distance that an advisor gives. Such investors can't spare the time, and they like to sleep. So if you need an advisor for one of those two reasons, then you should use one with DFA access. But as I've already said, given the wide availability of tilted products via ETFs, even that's not absolutely necessary. If you do use an advisor, pay no more than 50 basis points per year.

There is one way you can get access to DFA without paying for an advisor—at least directly—and that's participating in one of the increasing number of defined-contribution retirement plans that offer a limited menu of DFA funds. Moreover, although DFA frowns on the practice, it is occasionally possible to find independent advisors who will offer access, without much in the way of advice, for a relatively nominal fee.

For nearly two decades, DFA has tracked the performance of the following fixed-mix of stock asset classes ("recommended" is too strong a word to apply here). Although this mix refers to specific DFA funds, it can be applied to a tilted portfolio of open-end funds and ETFs from other families:

- 20% U.S. Large Market
- 20% U.S. Large Value
- 10% U.S. Microcap
- 10% U.S. Small Value
- 10% U.S. REIT
- 10% (Developed Nation) International Large Value
- 5% (Developed Nation) International Small
- 5% (Developed Nation) International Small Value
- 3% Emerging Markets Large Market
- 3% Emerging Markets Large Value
- 4% Emerging Markets Small

This is a pretty good starting point for an all-equity portfolio, moderately tilted towards the small and value factors. Regarding the other two factors, momentum and profitability, DFA—and presumably the ETF providers—are also tilting their portfolios towards these. But as I've previously mentioned, it's impossible to significantly and simultaneously tilt toward too many factors without severely restricting the universe of eligible securities.

Notice, though, that the DFA equity strategy has only 30% foreign exposure and contains no international REITs or a separate allocation to commodities/precious metals producing stocks. Given current valuations, a reasonable investing adult might increase the exposure to foreign (particularly to emerging markets) stocks, replace some of the domestic REITs with international ones, and add in a few percent of precious metals equity, especially given the dramatic recent price falls of the gold miners. Again, you're an investing adult, so I'm not going to spoon-feed you the numbers.

One last thing about DFA's fund strategies. They have evolved away from the "four corners" approach displayed above (large market, large value, small market, and small value) and have moved towards a one-fund solution: Core 1 (mildly tilted), Core 2 (moderately tilted), and Vector (highly tilted). If we consider their two vector funds (U.S. and developed international) to be "Core 3," then the U.S. and developed international small value portfolios can be viewed as "Core 4," or maximally tilted. To complicate things even further, tax-managed versions of some of these approaches are also available, as are ex-U.S. funds that combine, for purposes of tax efficiency, developed foreign and emerging markets. Again, tilt is tilt, and these core funds have a small transactional advantage over a component approach. This is because fewer companies have to be bought and sold as they cross the borders between the older four-corner pigeonholes. This small advantage has to be weighed against the loss of control over the fine-tuning of value/small loadings and of the benefit of rebalancing within the four corners.

Finally, DFA even offers the only all-in-one tilted stock mutual fund that passes passive muster: the Global Equity Portfolio, which approximates the balanced strategy above at roughly the Core 2 level of tilt. This is available in some defined contribution plans, and it's a fine way to package the entire risky part of a portfolio in a sheltered environment. DFA also offers a less well used fund, the Global Allocation 60/40 Portfolio, which adds in a high-quality short-term bond component. This fund well serves investors who want a simple, tilted, one-fund solution to retirement savings.

To repeat, tilt is tilt, no matter where it comes from. The standard way of determining the degree of portfolio tilt is to regress its returns against each of the risk factors. For example, over the 3-year period ending October 2013, the DFA U.S. Vector Fund had small/value loadings of 0.53/0.28. The same loading could have been approximated with a mix of roughly 40% total U.S. stock market (which by definition has loadings of 0.00/0.00) and 60% DFA U.S. Small Cap Value Portfolio, which had loadings of 0.92/0.39. Alternatively, a 40/60 mix of DFA U.S. Large Company Value Portfolio (loadings of 0.06/0.45) and U.S. Small Cap Portfolio (loadings of 0.90/0.19) would have accomplished roughly the same factor loading as the U.S. Vector Fund, as would a 20/20/30/30 traditional "four corners" mix of LM/LV/SM/SV.

If you want even more tilt than the DFA balanced approach listed above, you would increase the allocations to small value in the U.S. and developed markets. In emerging markets, the only fund that approximates small value exposure is the WisdomTree Emerging Markets SmallCap Dividend Fund. In tables 6-1, 6-2, and 6-3, I've listed fund choices for each stock asset class for the U.S. equity, international equity, and fixed-income asset classes, respectively.

Vanguard does offer a cap-weighted (that is, untilted) version of DFA's Global Equity Portfolio: the Total World Stock Index Fund. But I don't recommend it, for two reasons. First of all, as we discussed in chapter 2, a market-cap-weighted world equity fund is suboptimal for most U.S. investors. Since their consumption will be in dollars, at least a moderate amount of home-market bias is appropriate, and the current 48/52 domestic/foreign split of the world market cap that this fund reflects is too heavy on international stocks. Second, this fund's fees are uncharacteristically high for a Vanguard offering. The open-end fund is available only as Investor class shares, with a 0.35% expense ratio (ER). With a customized blend of U.S. and international total market funds, the same portfolio can be bought with Investor class shares at 0.17% and 0.22% of expense, respectively, and much more cheaply as Admiral class shares, which the Total World Stock Index Fund does not make available. Similarly, the ETF version of the Total World Stock Index Fund costs 0.17%, versus 0.05% and 0.16%, respectively, for the ETF versions of the U.S. and international total market funds.

Table 6-1. Recommended U.S. Equity Funds

Asset Class	Fund
U.S. Cap-Weighted	Vanguard Total Stock Market
U.S. Large-Cap Market	Vanguard Large-Cap Index
U.S. Large-Cap Value	Dimensional U.S. Large Cap Value Dimensional Tax-Managed U.S. Marketwide Value Vanguard Mid-Cap Value Index* Powershares FTSE RAFI U.S. 1000**
U.S. Small-Cap Market	Vanguard Small-Cap Index Vanguard Tax-Managed Small Cap Dimensional U.S. Microcap Dimensional Tax-Managed U.S. Small Cap
U.S. Small Value	Dimensional U.S. Small Cap Value Dimensional Tax-Managed U.S. Targeted Value Powershares FTSE RAFI U.S. Pure Small Value Index** Vanguard Small-Cap Value Index
U.S. Multifactor Core	Dimensional U.S. Core Equity 1 (mild tilt) Dimensional U.S. Core Equity 2 (moderate tilt) Dimensional Tax-Advantaged U.S. Core Equity 2 (moderate tilt) Dimensional U.S. Vector (high tilt)
REIT	Vanguard REIT Index
Commodity Producer	(Van Eck) Market Vectors Gold Miners** Vanguard Energy**

*The Vanguard Mid-Cap Value Index Fund is chosen in preference to the (Large-Cap) Value Index Fund because it corresponds more closely in behavior to the Dimensional and Powershares funds.

**ETF only.

Table 6-2. Recommended Foreign Equity Funds

Asset Class	Fund
Developed Regional	Vanguard European Stock Index Vanguard Pacific Stock Index
Developed Large-Cap Market	Vanguard Developed Markets Index
Developed Large-Cap Value	Dimensional International Value Dimensional Tax-Managed International Value Powershares FTSE RAFI Developed Markets ex-U.S.
Developed Small-Cap Market	Dimensional International Small-Company
Developed Small-Cap Value	Dimensional International Small Cap Value Powershares FTSE RAFI Developed Markets ex-U.S. Small-Mid
Developed Multifactor Core	Dimensional International Core Equity (moderate tilt) Dimensional International Vector Equity (high tilt)
Emerging Markets Large-Cap	Vanguard Emerging Markets Stock Index
Emerging Markets Large-Cap Value	Dimensional Emerging Markets Value Powershares FTSE RAFI Emerging Markets
Emerging Markets Small-Cap	Dimensional Emerging Markets Small Cap
Emerging Markets Small-Cap Value	Wisdom Tree Emerging Markets SmallCap Dividend
Emerging Markets Multifactor Core	Dimensional Emerging Markets Core Equity (moderate tilt)
Developed+Emerging Markets Large-Cap Market	Vanguard Total International Stock Index

Table 6-2. Continued

Developed+Emerging Markets Large-Cap Value	Dimensional World ex-U.S. Value
Developed+Emerging Markets Small-Cap Market	Vanguard FTSE All-World ex-U.S. Small-Cap Index
Developed+Emerging Markets Small-Cap Value	Dimensional World ex-U.S. Targeted Value
Developed+Emerging Markets Multifactor Core	Dimensional World ex-U.S. Core Equity (moderate tilt) Dimensional Tax-Advantaged World ex-U.S. Core Equity (moderate tilt)

Table 6-3. Recommended Vanguard Bond Funds

Municipal Bond Mutual Funds
(available as Investor and Admiral class shares)

Fund	Duration (years)
Short-Term Tax-Exempt	1.1
Limited-Term Tax-Exempt	2.3
Intermediate-Term Tax-Exempt	5.5
Long-Term Tax-Exempt	7.6
California Intermediate-Term Tax-Exempt	5.7
California Long-Term Tax-Exempt	7.6
Massachusetts Tax-Exempt*	7.3
New Jersey Long-Term Tax-Exempt	7.6
New York Long-Term Tax-Exempt	7.4
Ohio Long-Term Tax-Exempt*	7.7
Pennsylvania Long-Term Tax-Exempt	7.3

*Not available in Admiral class shares.

Total Bond Market Index Funds
(available as Investor and Admiral class shares)

Fund	Duration (years)
Short-Term Bond Index	2.7
Intermediate-Term Bond Index	6.5
Long-Term Bond Index*	14.0
Total Bond Index	5.5

*Not available in Admiral class shares.

Corporate Bond Index Funds
(available only as Admiral class shares and ETF)

Fund	Duration (years)
Short-Term Corporate Bond Index	2.8
Intermediate-Term Corporate Bond Index**	6.5
Long-Term Corporate Bond Index***	13.3

**0.25% purchase fee.
***1.00% purchase fee.

The Rebalancing Biz

The final aspect of nuts-and-bolts portfolio management deals with the when, how, and why of rebalancing. This has been a particular interest of mine over the past 20 years; in fact, it's the reason I first got seriously interested in finance.

Rebalancing is one of the thorniest questions in asset management. The return benefits of rebalancing, to the extent they exist at all, are relatively small—about half a percentage point per year. For example, in the late 1990s, I looked at a multitude of rebalancing intervals, ranging from 1 month to 4 years, for a 40/15/15/30 portfolio of S&P 500/U.S. small stocks/ EAFE/5-year Treasuries over a large number of staggered 28-year periods. The average portfolio returns increased with longer rebalancing intervals, but only slightly, from 1 month (12.030%) to 4 years (12.267%). In other words, there was less than a quarter of a percentage point difference between the best and worst strategies. At that level, the small difference would take centuries to reach statistical significance.

And that's just calendar rebalancing. Threshold rebalancing — that is, transacting only when given bounds are exceeded — is an even dicier proposition to evaluate, since it's an extremely chaotic system. Consider, for example, the 20%-plus drops in the major U.S. stock indexes on Black Monday, October 19, 1987. Whether or not you rebalanced on that day depended on your starting dates, starting allocations, *and* on the size of the threshold triggers. A small difference in any of these three variables determined whether you did or did not purchase a large amount of equity at that point, which in turn produced a large change in subsequent portfolio returns, certainly much larger than the relatively small differences in annualized return noted in the exercise above.

Because threshold rebalancing tends to "catch" market peaks and valleys more effectively than simple calendar rebalancing, I believe it is likely to be superior to calendar rebalancing. But since rebalancing is a very path-dependent process, I can't be sure. That said, certain rules should be followed.

Calendar rebalancing is still an effective, and quite simple, way to rebalance. If you use this method, do not rebalance more than once a year. Markets tend to exhibit momentum at periods of one year or less, and mean reversion takes place over longer periods. Rebalancing once every two to three years is plenty.

Threshold rebalancing is much trickier to do properly, and simple rules such as "Rebalance when your stock allocation or asset-class allocation exceeds or falls below policy, respectively, by 5%" make little sense. In the first place, thresholds should always be set as a percentage of the policy allocation. Let's start with the U.S. large cap component of a portfolio. A reasonable rebalancing threshold might be 20% of the allocation. Twenty percent of a 30% allocation is 6%, so you should rebalance back to target when this asset class hits 36%. Emerging markets are much more volatile, and so a wider threshold is called for here, perhaps 50%. If its policy allocation is 5%, then on the upside you'll rebalance at 7.5%.

On the downside, things are even trickier. Asset returns behave approximately lognormally. A 20% increase exactly offsets a 16.67% decline. A 50% increase offsets a 33.33% decline. Therefore, in the examples above, your targets on the downside should be 25% for U.S. large cap (30% x 0.8333; that is, 30% divided by 1.2), and 3.33% for emerging markets (5% x 0.6667; that is, 5% divided by 1.5). For each individual asset class, these thresholds are works in progress. If you wind up rebalancing an asset class more than once per year on average, you should widen your thresholds. If you're hardly rebalancing at all, narrow the thresholds. Your target should be to rebalance once every 2 to 4 years for each asset class.

Rebalancing versus Overbalancing (Strategic Asset Allocation)

Make no mistake about it. Maintaining even a constant asset allocation is hard enough, as the 2008–2009 financial crisis and the grisly "hyperbear market" of 1929–1932 well demonstrated. Both of these required disciplined investors to shovel their newly precious cash down what seemed a bottomless equity rat hole. Even harder is adjusting equity allocations up and down opposite valuation, which requires consuming even *more* of the cash that becomes especially valuable in a crisis.

In spite of the dubious data in support of manipulation of the overall stock and bond allocations with valuation measures such as the CAPE, those who reduced equity allocations in response to the 1990s tech bubble or the 2000s real-estate bubble (which spilled over into stocks) and who raised them, particularly abroad, in response to more reasonable valuations in 2002 and 2008–2009 were not disappointed. The data of Dimson, Marsh, and Staunton are highly suggestive that shifting allocations *among* equity asset classes according to valuation can be beneficial. Again, you did not have to be a genius to note during the tech bubble that the S&P 500 yield barely exceeded 1%, while various REIT indexes flirted with a 9% yield. Did anyone with rational expectations believe that the per-share dividends of the S&P 500 were going to grow 8% faster than the dividends of REIT indexes out to the horizon? Did any moderately intelligent investor believe that Japanese stocks selling at near-triple-digit multiples in the late 1980s were not a disaster waiting to happen?

Care, of course, should be taken in using the word "bubble." Of late, market observers have begun to bandy this term about a bit too liberally. As this is being written in early 2014, for example, the current CAPE of 25 is at about the 91st percentile of its historical range, which does not fit my concept of "bubble." Simply applying the two-term Gordon equation (dividend yield plus growth) suggests an expected real return of around 3.5%, which, while not great, is not awful either. On the other hand, in early 2000 the CAPE peaked at more than 44.2, which was well outside of previous historical bounds. The expected real return calculated at that time, 2.5%, was actually lower than the TIPS yield of 4%. (For the record, the 1st and 5th percentile boundaries of the CAPE are 42 and 27, respectively.)

The prime directive for strategic asset allocation is *small, infrequent changes in allocation opposite large changes in valuation.* For example, if the S&P 500 index has halved or doubled over the space of a few years, as it did, respectively, between 2007 and 2009 and between 2009 and 2012, it would not be inappropriate to, respectively, raise or lower the equity allocation by several percent. Over the past decade, the price level of precious metals equity (PME) stocks has gyrated wildly. In 2012 and 2013, they fell by more than half. If, and only if, you've had a disciplined long-term allocation to PME (i.e., you didn't buy in for the first time at high prices several years ago), it might not be a bad idea to now up your policy allocation to this asset class, which, it should be noted, is infamous for having negative real returns for decades at a time. A practical and conservative way to adjust allocations by price changes might be by, say, a 10-to-1 ratio on the upside and perhaps (because of the lognormal math) a 6-to-1 ratio on the downside.

In the short term, price changes will be almost precisely mirrored by valuation changes, which is why I recommend the above type of rule of thumb for most allocation adjustments. In the long run, though, you'll have to pay attention to more than just price changes, since doing so will eventually unmoor the allocation from fundamental valuations. The investing adult carefully monitors hard valuation data, and this can be problematic for the individual. The Shiller CAPE plot is easily available from the good professor's Yale Web site, and NAREIT.com maintains a data series of REIT dividend yields. The best way, more generally, to do this is to follow the P/E, P/B, and dividend yields of index funds. Vanguard lists these for its funds on its Web site. These metrics can be found, as well, at Morningstar.com, under the Portfolio tab of a particular fund's Web page.

If you're serious about this process, you'll check these metrics on a monthly or quarterly basis for a wide range of asset classes. Even better, start recording them for later reference. (Hint: the process using the Morningstar Web site can be tedious. To save time, once you've found the portfolio metrics page for any fund, you can quickly find it for another fund by changing the ticker symbol that is buried in the URL in the address bar of your Web browser. If you know someone with access to Morningstar Principia or to the Dimensional Web site data bank, you can also build a library of prior valuations.)

At the time of this writing, this sort of analysis shows that, in general, U.S. stocks are about as expensive as they were just before the Global Financial Crisis. Emerging markets stocks are nearly as cheap as they were in 2009, and developed markets stocks are in between these two extremes. This is useful information for the investing adult.

Final Words: Economics, Demographics, Risk, and You

I'll end with a somewhat woolly, but highly relevant discourse on the long-term evolution of return and risk throughout history. Most critically, returns on assets have been falling over the past several thousand years. There are three reasons for this.

First, as societies grow wealthier, the supply and demand balance of capital shifts in favor of its consumers (companies) and away from its providers (investors). Imagine a subsistence-level society plodding along at the precipice of starvation. Such a society has little excess capital—nearly every last basket of grain and every last piece of silver is consumed for food and shelter. But even subsistence societies need capital, particularly for seed, farm implements, and housing. In early agrarian societies, the cost of capital was high indeed. A rich farmer could lend his grain or livestock at a prodigious rate of interest—traditionally, a bushel of wheat or a calf paid twice over at harvest or calving time—a 100% return in less than a year.[1] (This "prehistoric interest rate" may be a bit of an overestimate because in the absence of advanced storage and transport facilities, grain will sell for greatly less at harvest time than it will at planting time.) As a society becomes more productive, wealth slowly accrues in the hands of the fortunate few with grain, domesticated animals, and silver to spare. Capital becomes more plentiful, not only in an absolute sense, but also relative to the need for it, as we have just seen. Although wealthy societies consume more capital than poor societies, with time, the balance of power slips away from investors.

Second, as societies grow wealthier, healthier, and longer-lived, investors become less hungry for consumption and are willing to accept a lower rate of return. Irving Fisher, probably the greatest economist of the early twentieth century, framed this quest with a far more down-to-earth term generations ago. Impatience, he called it.[2] In even plainer terms—a cheeseburger now or two tomorrow? Your indifference curve for cheeseburgers depends on how hungry you are at the moment and, to a lesser extent, on how healthy and well housed you are—in short, how impatient you are for the cheeseburger.

In the ancient and medieval worlds, starving and poorly housed people with short life expectancies were highly "impatient" for capital and consumption, and thus they demanded higher interest rates for their capital than do better-fed, better-housed, and longer-lived modern populations. But no matter how we explain things—whether in terms of impatience or as a function of the supply and demand status of capital—the effect is identical: The further the world population dwells above the subsistence level, the lower its cost of capital.

Third, recent advances in intermediation (that is, widely available index funds for just about any asset class you might want) have also raised prices, and thus reduced returns. Most finance books, including this one, treat historical market returns, such as those of the S&P 500 (which didn't even exist before 1951) rather glibly, as if they could be easily obtained by any investor. But before the advent of the first index funds in the mid-1970s, it was nearly impossible for an individual to maintain a well-diversified list of stocks, let alone invest in an entire universe of them. Given the high brokerage fees before "May Day" in 1975, it was also expensive to do so—even for the collection of dividends. As we saw in John Templeton's story in chapter 1, it's even more nonsensical to talk about the historical investment returns of small-cap stocks, almost all of which traded over the counter with astronomical spreads. When liquidity is low and purchase is difficult, share prices are necessarily lower, and expected returns higher, than when a passively managed portfolio of several hundred, or even several thousand, stocks can be purchased with the push of a button.

These are not theoretical considerations. As discussed above, in prehistoric or preliterate societies, the return on capital was about 100% per year. By remote antiquity, the return on well-secured loan capital was 10% to 20%. It then fell into the middle single digits by the sixteenth and seventeenth centuries in northern Europe. If we look at the returns on U.S. stocks over the past two centuries, we see that dividend yields have fallen from around 6% or so to 2%, with no significant increase in the dividend growth.[3]

The foregoing paints a fairly grim picture of life-cycle investing. The longer life spans (and thus longer retirements) and the low security returns seen in wealthy nations combine to deal a double blow to anyone dreaming of retiring in his or her 50s or even 60s. Such is the price of living in increasingly rich, safe, and rewarding societies. But who among us would trade this bargain for a world of rutted, bandit-infested roads, astronomical infant mortality, and no antibiotics?

Nonetheless, you're an investing adult, so you know all this. You can take solace in the knowledge that the overwhelming majority of investors aren't adults. You're almost certainly running faster than your cohorts being chased by the demographic and capital returns bears, so you likely won't get caught and eaten by them.

I'll end this book where I started in the Introduction, with Rabbi Hillel. Perhaps the Torah of finance turns out to be just a shade more complicated than risky and riskless assets, and having lots of the latter. But the fact that you've gotten this far means that you'll continue to study, which is a never-ending journey for the investing adult.

ACKNOWLEDGMENTS

I would like to thank John D'Antonio for editorial expertise, Nitasha Malhotra and Chetah Wagh at Reality Premedia for production services, Jason Zweig for editorial advice, Ed Tower for statistical support and theoretical guidance, Rick Ferri for sharing his deep knowledge of ETFs, Catherine Taylor for graphics assistance, and especially Elroy Dimson for providing me with long-run returns data and Ken French for allowing me to extensively quote his public database. Ed Chang, Steve Heller, Matt Henderson, Jerome Moisand, and Daniel Stern lent their eagle eyes to the manuscript.

And, as always, Jane Gigler deserves both thanks for her editorial assistance and appreciation for the saintly patience necessitated by a distracted husband.

NOTES

Introduction

1. "Philologos," "The Rest of 'The Rest is Commentary,'" *The Jewish Daily Forward*, September 24, 2008, http://forward.com/articles/14250/the-rest-of-the-rest-is-commentary-/, accessed March 20, 2013.
2. I, and the rest of the financial world, owe a debt of gratitude to Mr. Ilmanen for giving this concept voice in *Expected Returns* (Hoboken, NJ: John Wiley & Sons, 2012).

Chapter 1

1. Ilmanen, ibid.
2. Unfortunately, much of the evolving research in this area is proprietary. For an excellent summary of this area, see http://www.cbsnews.com/8301-505123_162-57480957/a-way-to-get-stock-like-returns-with-less-risk/ and http://www.advisorperspectives.com/newsletters13/Putting_GMOs_Ideas_to_Work.php.
3. Fred Schwed, *Where are the Customers' Yachts?* (Hoboken, NJ: John Wiley & Sons, 2006), 54.
4. André F. Perold and William F. Sharpe, "Dynamic Strategies for Asset Allocation," *Financial Analysts Journal* 44:1 (January/February, 1988): 16–27.
5. For an excellent summary of power-law relationships of terrorist attacks and earthquakes, see Nate Silver, *The Signal and the Noise* (New York: The Penguin Press, 2012), 149–72, 428–32. For meteoroid/asteroid strikes, see P. G Brown et al., "A 500-kiloton Airburst over Chelyabinsk and an Enhanced Hazard from Small Impactors," *Nature* 503 (November 14, 2013): 238–41. These authors, as well as those of the *Nature* piece, estimated the energy release

of the 2012 Chelyabinsk meteoroid at a half megaton of TNT and the 1908 Tunguska Event at about 5 megatons. Chelyabinsk-magnitude events are estimated to occur about once per century, Tunguska-magnitude events about once per millennium.

6. See, for example, http://www.efficientfrontier.com/ef/104/iid.htm and Xavier Gabaix et al., "Power Laws in Economics and Finance," *Annual Review of Economics* 1 (2009): 255–93.

7. Michelle Clayman, "In Search of Excellence: The Investor's Viewpoint," *Financial Analysts Journal* 54:3 (May/June, 1987): 54–63.

8. R. J. Fuller, L. C. Huberts, and M. J. Levinson, "Returns to E/P Strategies; Higgledy Piggledy Growth; Analysts Forecast Errors; and Omitted Risk Factors," *Journal of Portfolio Management* 19:2 (Winter, 1993): 13–24.

9. David N. Dreman and Michael A. Berry, "Overreaction, Underreaction, and the Low P/E Effect," *Financial Analysts Journal* 51:4 (May/June 1995): 21–30.

10. Eugene F. Fama and Kenneth R. French, "Size and Book-to-Market Factors in Earnings and Returns," *Journal of Finance* 50:1 (March, 1995), 131–55.

11. Madelon DeVoe Talley, *The Passionate Investors* (New York: Crown Publishing Inc., 1987), 66–69.

12. Philippe Jorion and William N. Goetzmann, "Global Stock Markets in the Twentieth Century," *Journal of Finance* 54:3 (June 1999): 953–80.

13. http://www.econ.yale.edu/~shiller/data/ie_data.xls.

14. Joe Weisenthal, "Goldman Sounds the Alarm on Stocks," *Business Insider* (January 13, 2014), http://www.businessinsider.com/goldman-market-valuation-is-lofty-2014-1, accessed March 25, 2014.

15. Eugene Fama and Kenneth French, op cit.

16. The computation of which stocks go in the upper and lower half by size (deciles 1-5 and 6-10), for example, is defined

by the companies in the New York Stock Exchange. So, for example, if 1,600 U.S. companies trade on the NYSE, then each decile starts with 160 companies. NASDAQ and American Stock Exchange companies are then added to each of those deciles according to which NYSE decile they fit into. The number of companies, thus, increases with smaller sized deciles. Decile 10 now has more than 2,000 names. Similar breakpoints are also established for foreign exchanges. The value factor is the average of the returns of long-short book-to-market portfolios set up for deciles 1-5 and 6-10. For a fuller description of how portfolios are broken down, see http://mba.tuck.dartmouth.edu/pages/faculty/ken.french/data_library.html#Breakpoints.

17. Andrei Schleifer and Robert W. Vishny, "The Limits of Arbitrage," *Journal of Finance* 51:1 (March, 1997): 35–55.

18. William J. Bernstein and Robert D. Arnott, "Earnings Growth: The Two Percent Dilution," *Financial Analysts Journal* 59:5 (September/October, 2003): 47–55.

19. Mebane T. Faber, "Global Value: Building Trading Models with the 10-Year CAPE," SSRN working paper, http://papers.ssrn.com/sol3/papers.cfm?abstract_id=489602.

20. Jason Zweig, "The Ron Paul Portfolio," *Wall Street Journal*, December 21, 2011. Full disclosure: In the piece, Mr. Zweig quoted this author describing Mr. Paul's portfolio as "a half step away from a cellar full of canned goods and nine-millimeter rounds." Both Mr. Zweig and this author were subsequently excoriated in the piece's Comments section. It should be noted that in the time since the article was written, the price of PME, as measured by the GDX indexed ETF, has declined by more than half.

21. William J. Bernstein, *Skating Where the Puck Was* (Portland, OR: Efficient Frontier Publications, 2012).

22. Ibid.

Chapter 2

1. Professor Kenneth French maintains an extensive library of constantly updated data on U.S. industry returns and international equity returns at http://mba.tuck.dartmouth.edu/pages/faculty/ken.french/data_library.html.

2. Ronald Balvers et al., "Mean Reversion across National Stock Markets and Parametric Contrarian Investment Strategies," *Journal of Finance* 55:2 (April, 2000), 745–72.

3. Harry Markowitz, "Portfolio Selection," *Journal of Finance* 7:1 (March, 1952), 77–91.

4. William J. Bernstein, *The Ages of the Investor* (Efficient Frontier Publications, 2012).

5. Robert B. Barsky et al., "Preference Parameters and Behavioral Heterogeneity: An Experimental Approach in the Health and Retirement Study," *Quarterly Journal of Economics* 112:2 (May, 1997): 540.

6. Ibid., 537–39.

7. Neal Templin, "Honey, I Shrunk the Nest Egg (And I'm Sorry)," *Wall Street Journal*, May 21, 2009.

8. Kent Daniel and Tobias Moskowitz, "Momentum Crashes," working paper, http://bus.miami.edu/umbfc/_common/files/papers/Daniel.pdf.

9. Robert Novy-Marx, "The Other Side of Value: Good Growth and the Gross Profitability Premium," NBER Working Paper 15940, April 2010.

10. Joe Nocera, "Poking Holes in a Theory on Markets," *New York Times*, June 5, 2009.

11. Samuel Jung and Robert J. Shiller, "Samuelson's Dictum and the Stock Market," Cowles Foundation Paper No. 1183 (New Haven, CT: Cowles Foundation for Research in Economics, 2006).

12. Meir Statman, unpublished work. The final version of Professor Statman's paper, "Efficient Markets in Crisis," *Journal of Investment Management* 9:2 (2011): 4–13, uses a

different formulation, which substitutes "informationally efficient" for "fair."

13. Ivo Welch and Amit Goyal, "A Comprehensive Look at the Empirical Performance of Equity Premium Prediction," *Review of Financial Studies* 21:4 (July, 2008), 1455–1508. The quote comes from p. 1455.

14. Elroy Dimson et al., *Triumph of the Optimists* (Princeton: Princeton University Press, 2002), see pp. 229–315 for detailed decade-by-decade returns for stocks, bonds, and bills, as well as inflation data for their nation database. For the past several years the authors have made available updates of their data, with much additional analysis, for free from Credit Suisse at

2010 Yearbook: http://tinyurl.com/DMS2010,

2011 Yearbook: http://www.scribd.com/doc/57347299/Credit-Suisse-Global-Investment-Yearbook-2011,

2012 Yearbook: https://www.credit-suisse.com/investment_banking/doc/cs_global_investment_returns_yearbook.pdf,

2013 Yearbook http://www.investmenteurope.net/digital_assets/6305/2013_yearbook_final_web.pdf,

2014 Yearbook https://publications.credit-suisse.com/tasks/render/file/?fileID=0E0A3525-EA60-2750-71CE20B5D14A7818.

15. A good summary of this controversy can be found in my interchange with Professor William Reichenstein on the subject at "Do Your Asset Classes Care Where They Are?" http://www.efficientfrontier.com/ef/704/where.htm.

Chapter 3

1. Johathan Cheng, "Mom and Pop Run with the Bulls," *Wall Street Journal*, March 29, 2013.

2. Baba Shiv et al., "Investment Behavior and the Negative Side of Emotion," *Psychological Science* 16:6 (June, 2005), 435–39.

3. Michael Lewis, *The Big Short* (New York: W.W. Norton & Company, 2010).
4. Jason Zweig, "Time to Take Stock of the Recent Market Rallies," *Wall Street Journal*, April 3, 2010.
5. Benjamin Roth, *The Great Depression: A Diary* (New York: Public Affairs, 2009), 21.
6. Ibid., 44.
7. Ibid., 116.
8. Quoted in http://www.forbes.com/2008/10/23/inflated-treasuries-stockholders-cz_bg_1023forbesarchive.html, accessed 12/17/13.
9. Vishny and Schleifer, op. cit.
10. Although most frequently ascribed to Yogi Berra or Mark Twain, this aphorism probably has its origins in Danish folk wisdom. See http://quoteinvestigator.com/2013/10/20/no-predict/.
11. The one exception to this was semaphore/smoke signaling systems, reserved throughout history for the most precious of information.
12. Isaiah Berlin, *The Proper Study of Mankind*, (New York: Farrar, Strauss, and Giroux, 1998), 436–98. The quote comes from p. 436.
13. Philip E. Tetlock, *Expert Political Judgment* (Princeton, NJ: Princeton University Press, 2005).
14. Jonathan Haidt, *The Righteous Mind* (New York: Vintage Books, Ltd., 2012), 94–108.
15. Tetlock, 49–88, 98. The quote comes from p. 63.
16. Jason Zweig, "Peter Bernstein interview," http://money.cnn.com/2004/10/11/markets/benstein_bonus_0411/, accessed 12/18/2013.
17. Ulricke Malmendier and Stefan Nagel, "Learning from Inflation Experiences," working paper, http://www.econ.as.nyu.edu/docs/IO/30895/nagel.pdf, accessed 12/18/2013.
18. See Frederick Taylor, *The Downfall of Money* (New York: Bloomsbury Press, 2013), and Adam Fergusson, *When Money Dies* (New York: Public Affairs, 2010).

Chapter 4

1. William P. Bengen, "Determining Withdrawal Rates Using Historical Data," *Journal of Financial Planning* (October 1994): 14–24.
2. http://janav.wordpress.com/2013/03/31/rate-of-return-single-family-homes/, accessed May 5, 2013.
3. Savings rates from Table 9.1, EBRI Databook on Employee Benefits, http://www.ebri.org/publications/books/?fa=databook, accessed   May 6, 2013.
4. From Figure 13, http://www.ebri.org/pdf/briefspdf/EBRI_IB_12-2012_No380.401k-eoy2011.pdf, accessed May 6, 2013.
5. Thornton Parker, *What if the Boomers Can't Retire?* (New York: Berrett-Koehler Publishers, 2002), and Robert D. Arnott and Anne Casscells, "Demographics and Capital Market Returns," *Financial Analysts Journal* 59:2 (March/April 2003): 20–29.
6. Samuel Crowther, "Everybody Ought to Be Rich: An Interview with John J. Raskob," *Ladies' Home Journal* (August 1929), 772.
7. Shiller's series is available at http://www.econ.yale.edu/~shiller/data/ie_data.xls.
8. Ian Ayres and Barry J. Nalebuff, "Life-cycle Investing and Leverage: Buying Stock on Margin Can Reduce Retirement Risk," (NBER working paper 14094, p. 23), accessible at http://papers.ssrn.com/sol3/papers.cfm?abstract_id=1139110.
9. Ian Ayres and Barry J. Nalebuff, *Life-cycle Investing* (New York: Basic Books, 2010).
10. For a brief survey of the risk tolerance/age literature, see Nancy Ammon Jianakoplos and Alexandra Bernasek, "Financial Risk Taking by Age and Birth Cohort," *Southern Economic Journal* 72, no. 4 (April 2006): 981–1001; William B. Riley Jr. and K. Victor Chow, "Asset Allocation and Risk Aversion," *Financial Analysts Journal* 48, no. 6 (November–

December 1992): 32–37; Hui Wang and Sherman Hanna, "Does Risk Tolerance Decrease with Age?" *Financial Counseling and Planning* 8, no. 2 (1997): 27–31; and R.A. Morin and A.F. Suarez, "Risk Aversion Revisited," *Journal of Finance* 38, no. 4 (September 1983), 1201–16.

11. Michael Zwecher, *Retirement Portfolios* (Hoboken NJ: John Wiley & Sons, 2010).

12. Richard H. Thaler and Eric J. Johnson, "Gambling with the House Money and Trying to Break Even: The Effects of Prior Outcomes on Risky Choice," *Management Science* 36:6 (June, 1990): 643–60.

Chapter 5

1. If you've not listened to Ken French's 2008 American Finance Association presidential address, you're in for a treat: http://www.afajof.org/details/video/2870801/2008-Presidential-Address.html.

2. Richard Bookstaber, *A Demon of our Own Design* (Hoboken, NJ: John Wiley & Sons, 2008).

3. Charles Perrow, *Normal Accidents* (Princeton, NJ: Princeton University Press, 1984).

4. "Findings Regarding the Market Events of May 6, 2010," SEC, September 30, 2010, accessed November 19, 2013 at http://www.sec.gov/news/studies/2010/marketevents-report.pdf.

5. "Keeping Watch," *Economist* (November 23, 2013), accessed November 28, 213 at http://www.economist.com/news/special-report/21590099-economic-success-has-given-china-greater-weight-not-nearly-enough-tip?fsrc=rss l spr.

6. Larry Speidell et al., "Dilution is a Drag . . . The Impact of Financings in Foreign Markets," *Journal of Investing* 14:4 (Winter 2005):17–22.

7. William J. Bernstein and Robert D. Arnott, "The Two-Percent Dilution," *Financial Analysts Journal* (Sept.-Oct. 2003): 47–55.

8. Speidell et al., ibid.

9. DMS 2014 yearbook, op cit.

10. Credit Suisse 2013 Yearbook http://www.investmenteurope. net/digital_assets/6305/2013_yearbook_final_web.pdf, accessed July 20, 2013, see graphs on country pages.

11. Dimson, op. cit.

12. Philippe Jorion and William N. Goetzmann, "Global Stock Markets in the Twentieth Century," *Journal of Finance* 54:3 (June 2002): 953–80. A working version of the paper is available at https://faculty.fuqua.duke.edu/~charvey/ Teaching/IntesaBci_2001/GJ_Global.pdf. Their data showed approximately 3% price-only returns for Chile and Israel, to which I have added 4% to 5% dividends.

13. John Maynard Keynes, *General Theory of Employment, Interest and* Money (New Delhi: Atlantic Publishers, 2006), 345. Keynes, though, was not referring to inflation, but rather to confiscation.

14. William J. Bernstein, *Deep Risk* (Portland OR: Efficient Frontier Publications, 2013).

Chapter 6

1. Sidney Homer and Richard Sylla, *A History of Interest Rates,* 4th ed., (Hoboken, NJ: John Wiley & Sons, Inc., 2005), 21–23.

2. Irving Fisher, *The Theory of Interest* (Philadelphia: Porcupine Press, 1977).

3. William J. Bernstein, "The Paradox of Growth," *Financial Analysts Journal* 69:5 (September-October, 2013): 18–25.

INDEX

CPSIA information can be obtained
at www.ICGtesting.com
Printed in the USA
LVHW082002301122
734143LV00014B/645